ZHANG YIMOU

INTERVIEWS

CONVERSATIONS WITH FILMMAKERS SERIES
PETER BRUNETTE, GENERAL EDITOR

D1615795

Courtesy of Photofest

ZHANG
YIMOU

INTERVIEWS
EDITED BY FRANCES GATEWARD

UNIVERSITY PRESS OF MISSISSIPPI / JACKSON

www.upress.state.ms.us

Copyright © 2001 by University Press of Mississippi
All rights reserved
Manufactured in the United States of America

09   08   07   06   05   04   03   02   01   4   3   2   1

∞

Library of Congress Cataloging-in-Publication Data

Zhang Yimou : interviews / edited by Frances Gateward.
        p.   cm.—(Conversations with filmmakers series)
      Includes index.
      ISBN 1-57806-261-6 (alk. paper)—ISBN 1-57806-262-4 (pbk. : alk. paper)
      1. Zhang, Yimou—Interviews.   2. Motion picture producers and
directors—China—Interviews.   I. Gateward, Frances K.   II. Series.

PN1998.3.Z49 A5   2001
791.43'0233'092—dc21   00-068527

British Cataloging-in-Publication Data available

CONTENTS

INTRODUCTION

RARELY IN THE HISTORY of film has a single director come to be so thoroughly associated with an entire national output as Zhang Yimou[1] has been with contemporary Chinese cinema. Though he was by no means alone in introducing Chinese cinema to the world, Zhang's films have captured international attention, awards, and acclaim far in excess of his cohorts in Chinese cinema today. Certainly, he has been the most prolific of today's Chinese filmmakers, directing nine major films since his debut in 1987, and he has been, arguably, the most controversial, both at home and abroad. His seven films with actress Gong Li have led to comparisons with the likes of Josef von Sternberg, Jean-Luc Godard, and Ingmar Bergman in their use of Marlene Dietrich, Anna Karina, and Liv Ullmann, respectively, in numerous films and a similar romantic linking off screen. His sometimes leisurely pacing—the long-take-long-shot method—his pictorial compositions, and impressionistic use of color have singled him out as one of the premiere film directors not only of his day but in world cinema history.

Previously the province of only the most specialized scholars and cineastes, Chinese cinema experienced an unprecedented rebirth and international attention with the works of Zhang Yimou and his compatriots who graduated from the Beijing Film Academy in 1982. Quickly termed the "Fifth Generation" of Chinese cinema (these new filmmakers comprising the fifth graduating class of the Directing Department), these renaissance Chinese filmmakers not only put Chinese cinema back on the track of world-class film production, but also were instrumental in inaugurating a series of international co-productions and in generally bringing China to the attention of a world eager to learn more of this nation, which contains almost one quarter of the world's population. Zhang Yimou was singularly instrumental in this rebirth, acting as cinematographer for the initial releases of the Fifth Generation's films, including *One and Eight* (*Yige he bage*, Zhang Junzhao, 1983), *Yellow Earth* (*Huang tudi*, Chen Kaige, 1984) and *The Big Parade* (*Da yue bing*, Chen Kaige, 1986). His maiden directorial effort, *Red Sorghum* (*Hong gao liang*, 1987), took the Golden Bear at the Berlin Film Festival in 1988, validating the world-class status of Chinese cinema and putting Zhang on a path of international award-winning efforts.

But Zhang's path to world-cinema acclaim was a far from easy one. Born near Xi'an in 1951, Zhang came from a problematic background according to the Communist authorities.[2] His mother was a professional woman, a dermatologist, his father was chronically under-employed and under suspicion as a former officer in the Nationalist army (the Kuomintang or KMT) before the Communist victory in 1949. Sent—as many urban or educated youth—to the country during the Cultural Revolution, Zhang worked in agricultural and industrial jobs, though he developed an interest in still photography that later helped him gain entry to the Beijing Film Academy. Still lacking the political bona fides of many of his classmates, upon graduation from the academy Zhang was sent to the provincial film studio in Guangxi in far southeastern China. This proved highly advantageous—for he was placed far from the watchful eye of the authorities in Beijing and was not under the thumb of already established directors (the forced hiatus of filmmaking during the Cultural Revolution was, oddly, an important underpinning of the immediate access to directing experienced by the Fifth Generation filmmakers). Young filmmakers found the freedom to create small, but effective movies which would help revolutionize Chinese cinema. Zhang, as cinematographer, teamed up with director Zhang Junzhao and production designer He Qun to make *One and Eight*. Though it ran into some post-production scrutiny by the censorship authorities, it was eventually released to great domestic acclaim. Following this success, Zhang Yimou persuaded his friend and former classmate Chen Kaige to apply for reassignment from Beijing to Guangxi. Along with He Qun, they soon made *Yellow Earth*, which was an unqualified success at the 1985 Hong Kong International Film Festival and a qualified and controversial success at home. Zhang quickly developed a reputation as an innovative cinematographer based on the success of these two films. At the request of director and Xi'an Studio head Wu Tianming,

Zhang both starred in and shot Wu's *Old Well*, which furthered Zhang's budding reputation. He even won a Best Actor award at the Tokyo International Film Festival for his work in 1987. But certainly it would be his work as a director which would net Zhang the kind of international acclaim that no Chinese director had ever experienced.

Wu Tianming, as head of the Xi'an Studio, had instituted a policy of giving opportunities to young directors.[3] Thus it was that Zhang got his first directorial opportunity at Xi'an, and the result of which, *Red Sorghum*, led to Zhang's solidification as a director. It was also the first time he directed actress Gong Li. The film's considerable success in the domestic market and its overseas acclaim led Zhang to feel a good deal of commercial pressure, and his next film, an action-thriller entitled *Code Name Puma* (*Daihao meizhoubao*, 1988), was by all accounts a disaster. However, his next film, still at Xi'an Studio and again with Gong Li, was the film that established his overseas reputation as China's premier international director: *Ju Dou* (1990). Nominated for an Academy Award for Best Foreign Language Film and winner of the Golden Palm for Best Director at Cannes, *Ju Dou* was the first in a string of critical, commercial, and controversial successes. *Raise the Red Lantern* (*Dahong denglong gaogao gua*, 1991) followed suit with the Academy Award for Best Foreign Language Film and the Silver Lion for Best Film at the Venice Film Festival. *The Story of Qiu Ju* (*Qiu Ju da guan si*, 1992) again took the Silver Lion at Venice.

Zhang's initial directorial efforts can be seen in conjunction with many of the early films of the Fifth Generation directors. An intense self-examination is clearly underway, and while many of the same themes and motifs of 1930s and 1950s Chinese cinema are utilized, they are cast in a new light, a more critical light to be sure. Films such as *One and Eight, Yellow Earth,* and *Red Sorghum* continue the process of mythicizing the Chinese experience in World War II fighting the Japanese begun in the 1930s. Another common trend of his films, most based on works of Chinese literature, is the focus on female protagonists, women who often embody the nation-state. Thus he is often compared to the classical Japanese director Mizoguchi Kenji, who is sometimes seen as a director with feminist concerns. In his early works, pre-Revolutionary China is a favorite topic, especially the oppression of capitalist-patriarchy. While in the later half of his ongoing career, he has moved toward critiquing bureaucracy and materialism in more contemporary contexts. His more recent films also reflect a change in style.

The films upon which he built his reputation, *Red Sorghum, Ju Dou,* and *Raise the Red Lantern* were built upon stunning images with sumptuous color, languid cinematography, and the use of the static long takes. *The Story of Qiu Ju* (1993) was a major turning point for Zhang because it reflected a change in both form and content. This film, which he describes as being, "about a woman who comes to recognize her own self-worth" (see the interview with Yang), was his first set in contemporary times, the first with multiple comedic moments, and the first to stray from his established visual style. Shot entirely on location in the small village where Zhang grew up, in the province of Shaanxi, the film features a documentary aesthetic. The stars of the film were the only professional actors. They interacted with local villagers, often in front of hidden cameras. The setting was a departure from the symbolic claustrophobic and confining architecture of his early films, instead using open spaces and vast landscapes. Several years later, he used a similar approach in *Not One Less* (1999), using a cast of ordinary villagers and city dwellers, most of whom play themselves. Though visually austere, the film fits well in his oeuvre, for it is rich with character and emotion, focusing on the heroism of a thirteen-year-old primary school graduate who must serve as a substitute teacher.

Zhang Yimou, in only a little over a decade, has firmly established himself as one of the most important directors in film history. Clearly a genius of modern cinema, he has, as Sheldon Lu points out, "brought about a permanent change in the pattern of Chinese national cinema. After Zhang Yimou, the mechanisms of funding, production, marketing, distribution, and consumption of Chinese cinema were forever changed."[4] But his success has not been without cost. As we see in these interviews, Zhang has had to contend with a lack of creative freedom, hampered by government censors, fundraising difficulties, the inability to interact with international colleagues, and criticism accusing him of exoticizing Chinese culture for the pleasure of Westerners. Despite these obstacles Zhang Yimou remains a passionate and committed filmmaker, a complex, multi-talented, and modest individual, who seeks only to practice his art and to bring to the screen reflections of humanity and life in an ever-changing China.

Special recognition must be given to Yiu Yan Ling and Leung Wai Yee of the University of Hong Kong, without whom this book would not have been possible. Thanks Verdy and Zero! To my translators Stephanie Deboer and

Lenute Guikin, much appreciation for all your hard work. Thanks also to David Desser and Poshek Fu at the University of Illinois, Yeh Yueh-Yu of Hong Kong Baptist University, and Chris Berry of University of California–Berkeley for their generous assistance, and to the series editor Peter Brunette, who suggested a volume on Zhang.

Endnotes

1. Name order is rendered in the traditional Chinese fashion, family name first and given name second.

2. This is adapted from the appendix in Chris Berry, ed., *Perspectives on Chinese Cinema* (London: BFI, 1991), 201.

3. For further details on the origins of the Fifth Generation see Tony Rayns "Breakthroughs and Setbacks" in Chris Berry, ed., *Perspectives on Chinese Cinema* (London: BFI, 1992), 104–13.

4. For further information see Sheldon Lu "National Cinema, Cultural Critique, Transnational Capital: The Films of Zhang Yimou" in Sheldon Lu, ed., *Transnational Chinese Cinemas: Identity, Nationhood, Gender* (Honolulu: U of Hawaii P, 1997), 109.

CHRONOLOGY

1951   Born in the Shaanxi region of China on 14 November.

1966   Cultural Revolution erupts and secondary education is suspended.

1969   Sent to work on a farm, then for seven years as a laborer in a spinning mill. During this time he takes up painting and photography.

1974   Buys his first camera. Several of his photographs are published in local periodicals, including the *Shaanxi Daily*.

1979   Applies for the Beijing Film Academy and is rejected. After making a personal appeal to the Minister of Culture he is accepted.

1982   Graduates from the Academy and is assigned to Guangxi Film Studio.

1984   Works as cinematographer on *One and Eight*, the first feature made by a member of the Fifth Generation (Zhang Junzhao). He also works as the cinematographer on *Yellow Earth*, directed by Chen Kaige.

1985   Works with Chen again, as the cinematographer for *The Big Parade*. He performs as an actor in the *Old Well* and wins the Best Actor Award at the Tokyo Film Festival.

1987   *Red Sorghum* is released.

1988   *Red Sorghum* wins the Golden Bear at the Berlin Film Festival.

1989   Directs *Operation Cougar* (also known as *Operation Puma*).

1990   *Ju Dou*, produced by Tokuma Enterprise, a Japanese entertainment, group is released but banned in China because of its sexual content. In the West it is nominated for an Oscar, but Zhang is not permitted to attend. The film is awarded the Luis Buñuel Award at the Cannes Film Festival and is also nominated for the Palme d'Or at Cannes.

1991   *Raise the Red Lantern,* funded by Taiwanese money channeled through a Hong Kong subsidiary, is released but banned in China. The film is nominated for an Oscar (as a Hong Kong entry) for Best Foreign Film and for Best Foreign Film by the Independent Spirit Awards. The film wins Best Cinematography and Best Foreign Film from the National Society of Film Critics, Best Foreign Film from the New York Film Critics Circle, Best Cinematography from the Los Angeles Film Critics Association, the British Academy Award for the Best Film Not in the English Language, and the Silver Lion at the Venice Film Festival.

1992   Previous films *Ju Dou* and *Raise the Red Lantern* are "unbanned" in China. He makes *The Story of Qiu Ju,* which is recognized at the Venice Film Festival. It is awarded the Golden Lion, and Gong Li gets the Volpi Cup for Best Actress.

1993   *The Story of Qiu Ju* is nominated for Best Foreign Film by the Independent Spirit Awards and wins Best Foreign Language Film from the National Society of Film Critics.

1994   New film *To Live* wins at Cannes, with actor Ge You taking the prize for Best Actor, while the film wins the Jury Grand Prize. The film also wins at the British Academy Awards for Best Film Not in the English Language.

1995   *Shanghai Triad* is released and receives a nomination for the Palme d'Or. It wins the Technical Grand Prize at Cannes and is nominated for the Golden Globe Award for Best Foreign Language Film; cinematographer Lu Yue is nominated for an Oscar for Best Cinematography and wins the Los Angeles Film Critics Association Award and the New York Film Critics Circle Award. Zhang directs a short included in the film *Lumière and Company.*

1997   *Keep Cool* is released and unexpectedly withdrawn from Cannes by the Chinese government. The film is nominated for the Grand Jury Prize at the Los Angeles International Film Festival and the Golden Lion at Venice.

1999   *Not One Less* wins Best Feature at the Sao Paulo International Film Festival, the Golden Lion at the Venice Film Festival, and the Five Continents Award from the European Film Awards. Wei Minzhi is recognized by the Young Artists Awards with the Award for Best Performance in an International Film-Young Performer.

1999   *The Road Home,* nominated for the Golden Bear at the Berlin Film Festival, wins the Silver Bear and the Prize of the Ecumenical Jury.

FILMOGRAPHY

As Director

1987
RED SORGHUM/HONG GAOLIANG
Xi'an Film Studio
Producers: Wu Tian-Ming
Director: **Zhang Yimou**
Screenplay: Chen Jianyu and Zhu Wei, from the books by Mo Yan *Red Sorghum* and *Sorghum Wine*
Cinematography: Gu Changwei
Editing: Du Yuan
Production Design: Cao Juiping
Music: Zhao Jiping
Cast: Gong Li (Grandma), Teng Jiangen (Grandpa), Teng Rujun (Uncle Luohan), Ji Cunhua (Bandit), Jiu Ji (Son)
Color
91 minutes

1988
CODENAME COUGAR/CODENAME PUMA/DAIHAO MEIZHOUBAO
Xi'an Film Studio
Director: **Zhang Yimou**
Screenplay: Cheng Shiqing

Cinematography: Gu Changwei and Yang Lun
Production Design: Cao Jiuping and Tong Huamiao
Music: Guo Feng
Cast: Tian Min, Gong Li, Xu Yao, Yu Rongguang, Liu Xiaoning

1989
JU DOU
Xi'an Film Studio/Tokuma Communications Company
Producer: Hu Jian, Yokuma Yasuyochi, and Zhang Wenze
Director: **Zhang Yimou**
Writer: Lui Heng
Cinematography: Gu Changwei and Yang Lun
Editing: Du Yuan
Production design: Cao Juioing and Xian Rujin
Music: Xia Rujin and Zhao Jiping
Cast: Gong Li (Ju Dou), Wei Li (Yang Gin Shan), Li Baotian (Tian-qing)
Color
95 minutes

1991
RAISE THE RED LANTERN/DAHONG DENGLONG GAOGAO GUA
ERA International/Salon Productions/China Film
Producer: Chiu Fu-Sheng
Director: **Zhang Yimou**
Screenplay: Ni Zhen, from the novel *Wives and Concubines* by Su Tong
Cinematography: Zhao Fei
Music: Zhao Jiping
Editing: Du Yuan
Cast: Gong Li (Songlian), Kong Lin (Yan'er), Ma Jingwu (Chen Zuoqian), Cao Cuifen (Zhuoyun), Jin Shuyuan (Yuru), He Saifei (Meishan)
Color
125 minutes

1992
THE STORY OF QIU JU
Sil-Metropole/Beijing Film Academy—Youth Film Studio
Producer: Ma Fung Kwok and Feng Yiting

Director: **Zhang Yimou**
Screenplay: Liu Heng, from the novel *The Wan Family's Lawsuit* by Chen Yuanbin
Cinematography: Chi Xiaoning, Lu Hongyi, Yu Xiaoqun
Production Design: Cao Juiping
Editing: Du Yuan
Music: Zhao Jiping
Cast: Gong Li (Qiu Ju), Liu Peiqi (Qing-Lai), Lei Laosheng (Village Head), Yang Liuchun (Meizi), Ge Zhijun (Officer Li)
Color
110 minutes

1994
TO LIVE/HUOZHE
ERA International/Shanghai Film Studio
Producer: Chiu Fu-Sheng, Kow Funhong, Tseng Christophe
Director: **Zhang Yimou**
Screenplay: Wei Lu and Yu Hua (author of the novel)
Cinematography: Lu Yue
Production Design: Cao Jiuping
Editing: Du Yuan
Music: Zhao Jiping
Cast: Ge You (Fugui), Gong Li (Jiazhen), Niu Ben (Town Chief), Guo Tao (Chunsheng)
Color
125 minutes

1995
SHANGHAI TRIAD/YAO A YAO YAO DAO WAIPO GIAO
Shanghai Film Studios/Alpha Films
Producer: Wang Wei, Zhu Yonde, Wu Yigong, Yves Marmion
Director: **Zhang Yimou**
Screenplay: Bi Feiyu and Li Xian, adapted from the novel *Gang Law*
Cinematography: Lu Yue
Production Design: Cao Juiping
Editing: Du Yuan
Music: Zhang Guangtian

Cast: Gong Li (Xiao Jingbao), Li Baotian (Tang), Wang Xiaoxiao (Shuisheng), Li Xuejian (Sixth Uncle), Sun Chun (Song), Jiang Baoying (Cuihua)
Color
109 Minutes

LUMIÈRE ET COMPAGNIE/LUMIÈRE AND COMPANY
Zhang Yimou directed one short segment of this omnibus film.

1997
KEEP COOL/YOUHUA HAOHAO SHUO
Guangxi Film Studio
Producer: Wang Qiping
Director: **Zhang Yimou**
Screenplay: Ping Shu
Cinematography: Yue Lu
Production Design: Cao Juiping
Editing: Yuan Du
Music: Zang Tianshuo
Cast: You Ge (Policeman), Wen Jiang (Bookseller), Li Baotian (Lao Zhang), Tian Tian (Chen Xiaohua), Ying Qu (An Hong), **Zhang Yimou** (Junk Peddler)
Color
90 minutes

1999
NOT ONE LESS/YIGE DOU BUNENG SHAO
Guangxi Film Studio
Producer: Zhang Wieping and Zhao Yu
Director: **Zhang Yimou**
Screenplay: Shi Xiansheng
Cinematography: Hou Yong
Production Design: Cao Jiuping
Editing: Ru Zhai
Music: San Bao
Cast: Minzhi Wei (Wei Minzhi), Huike Zhang (Zhang Huike), Zhenda Tian (Village Chief), Enman Gao (Teacher Gao), Zhimei Sun (Sun Zhimei), Yuying Feng (TV Receptionist), Fanfan Li (TV Host)
Color
106 minutes

THE ROAD HOME/WO DE FU QIN MU QIN
Distributed by: Guanxi Film Studio
Producers: Zhang Weiping and Zhao Yu
Director: **Zhang Yimou**
Screenplay: Bao Shi
Cinematography: Yong Hou
Production Design: Cao Juiping
Editing: Zhai Ru
Music: Bao San
Cast: Zhang Ziyi (Young Zhao Di), Sun Hongiei (Luo Yusheng), Zheng Hao
(Luo Changyu), Zhao Yuelin (Old Zhao Di), Li Bin (Grandmother)
Color
89 minutes

As Cinematographer

One and Eight/Yige he bage (1983)
Yellow Earth/Huang tudi (1984)
Old Well/Lao jing (1986)
The Big Parade/Da yue bing (1986)

As Producer

Dragon Town Story/Lung sing jing yuet (1997)

As Writer

Soul of a Painter/Hua hun (1993)

As Actor

Old Well/Lao jing (1986)
Red Sorghum/Hong gao liang (1987)
A Terracotta Warrior/Qin yong (1989)
Keep Cool/You hua hao hao shuo (1997)

As Director for Television

Turnadot – At the Forbidden City of Bejing (1999)

ZHANG YIMOU

INTERVIEWS

Discussing *Red Sorghum*

JIAO XIONGPING/1988

Winning Credit for My Grandpa

Could you discuss how you chose the novel for Red Sorghum?
I didn't know Mo Yan; I first read his novel, *Red Sorghum,* really liked it, and then gave him a phone call. Mo Yan suggested that we meet once. It was April and I was still filming *Old Well,* but I rushed to Shandong—I was tanned very dark then and went just wearing tattered clothes. I entered the court-yard early in the morning and shouted at the top of my voice, "Mo Yan! Mo Yan!" A door on the second floor suddenly opened and a head peered out: "Zhang Yimou?" I was dark then, having just come back from living in the countryside; Mo Yan took one look at me and immediately liked me—people have told me that he said Yimou wasn't too bad, that I was just like the work unit leader in his village. I later found out that this is his highest standard for judging people—when he says someone isn't too bad, that someone is just like this village work unit leader. Mo Yan's fiction exudes a supernatural quality "cobblestones are ice-cold, the air reeks of blood, and my grandma's voice reverberates over the sorghum fields." How was I to film this? There was no way I could shoot empty scenes of the sorghum fields, right? I said to Mo Yan, we can't skip any steps, so why don't you and Chen Jianyu first write a literary script. At that time, I was busy filming *Old Well* and didn't have the time to worry about it; I also hoped Mo Yan could make a little profit for his writing. Later on would come the film script, and after that he

From *Turbulent Meeting: Dialogues with Contemporary Chinese Film* (Taiwan: Yuanliu Publishing, 1999). Translated by Stephanie Deboer.

wouldn't have to worry about it. Film, you know, must always be made
filmic.

Later on, Mo Yan wrote a letter to someone else, who passed it on to me
to read. I was really touched. He said he didn't care how the director shot the
film at all. Some writers are no good; they'll hold up their books and question
how you could have neglected to film this sentence—this sentence is so profound, so important! I really applauded Mo Yan when I read his letter. He
really understands that film is film. After he'd seen it, he even told me that
the film was a bit better and also said that from then on I only had to say the
word, and he'd let me film his fiction.

The overall form of Red Sorghum *seems to have avoided the detachment of Fifth
Generation directors and also preserved characteristics of traditional popular
drama.*
I think this is true. I've been conscious of this throughout my creation of the
film. I myself thought of it in terms of form and didn't actually consider the
box office too much. But I do feel that every director hopes that more people
will enjoy seeing a film. Regardless of whether you make an argument, talk
of an idea, or communicate a thought, you hope more people will accept it,
yet be imperceptibly influenced by it—you don't want to put everything on
the surface.

Red Sorghum really hopes to link these two aspects of film. On the whole,
I think that *Yellow Earth, Horse Thief,* and *King of the Children* have already
displayed this kind of film, with a reduced sense of theatricality, a striking
expression of ideas and feelings—their plots are rather "thin"—and of anti-
traditionalist construction. I think that over the past three to five years,
there's been no lack of this kind of work domestically and I didn't want to
repeat this pattern.

But the other, theatrical kinds of films don't take notice of film's means of
expression. They don't fully utilize the creativity of sight and sound and just
continuously knead things like dramatic conflict, theatrical principles, and
the climax. There are many films like this; they have flooded the market. So
I considered this in terms of form, blending and synthesizing the two together. It has a good story framework that's easy to follow, yet we were also
able to maintain our strengths as young filmmakers, bringing the characteristics of film language into full play and using our own methods to tell a
story.

Also, we wanted to reveal our thoughts and ideas in a natural and relaxed manner. There are many truths in this world. And actually, film is an artistic process. I've always felt that there's no need to use the screen to display profound truths—let philosophers deal with that. The most profound truths of the world are perhaps the simplest—finished in a sentence. *Red Sorghum* of course wants to discuss some truths and ideas but hopes that they'll be accepted easily and be more appealing. What the audience comes to understand in this process is their own business. I rather admire works into which ideas and philosophies blend and seep naturally—these are good films. What they say is very succinct and not so complicated. It's tiring to watch a film that isn't clear about what it says.

Mo Yan's fiction really has literary charm. His language manipulates ambiguities of contrast and juxtapositions of myth and reality; his structure is also complicated, continuously interweaving different points of view. The methods of your film seem to simplify it into a prototype of the book.
That's exactly right. I feel that film has to find its own means of expression; it can't duplicate literature. Even an adaptation of a good literary work must first become a film; it can't be a copy of literature. An adaptation doesn't have to be like the original work, and it should be filmic. The first thing I do is simplify its events—simplify and popularize them. Film goes by only once, and its form of viewing is compelling. There's no time to go back, or turn back and reflect. You have no choice but to go along with the screen. Sometimes in literary language one or two sentences are very refined and charming. You can repeatedly try to figure them out, and once you've reached the last chapter, you could even rummage back to reflect on earlier points in the book. A film goes by only once, and not many ordinary people will see it two or three times. The rest of the viewing space is black and silent—the only thing with light and sound is the screen. The audience has no choice but to move along with the film's time, and because of this, films shouldn't be too complicated. In adapting *Red Sorghum* to the screen, we had to select the events that went on without any interruption, were simple and succinct, and went by in one breath in the hopes of creating one overall kind of feeling— its very different from literature.

I noticed that the film consciously utilizes the visual language of Fifth Generation directors.

It basically continues this kind of language. We've rather emphasized narrative methods; we're comparatively filmic. The early period of Chinese film was influenced by the modern dramatic stage, and older generations of filmmakers stressed plot and events. We filmed it very differently, continuing the methods of a younger generation of directors.

Did you have any particular designs in terms of visuality and language?
Many. I feel that the visual impact created by *Red Sorghum*'s screen is very intense, and cinematography plays the most prominent role in controlling this. I myself am a cinematographer, and Gu Changwei is a first-rate one—there's no doubt about this. We're both excellent cinematographers—I'd say I'm one too, I won't be modest, but I really feel that I can't compare with Gu Changwei—and the movie definitely has intense visuality because of this. We stressed color—gave full reign to the use of it—and largely utilized red to the point where the whole last frame was all red. This sense of color is very striking. The symbolic meaning of red in China is implicitly understood by everyone; it's recently been used to represent revolution, but how long has this revolution been in China? In China's five thousand years of cultural tradition, the color red has simply represented hot passion, the approach of the sun, burning fire, warm blood. I think that for all humankind, it has a kind of intense feeling. You could never say that it was cool, could you?

To say it simply, through the strange events of a man and a woman in a sorghum field, it conveys a passionate attitude toward living, an unrestricted vitality of life, an enthusiasm, and an emotionally spirited attitude toward human life. Red was definitely the most appropriate color and could be used in great quantity to maintain a visual impact.

Is this experimentation with color inherited from Yellow Earth?
Yellow Earth was an attempt at this, but its premises were different. It was more a critique and reflection—through historical introspection and the slow, steady, and immutable rhythms of life—on the nation and history. You see, the use of color in *Yellow Earth* is controlled. In this vast piece of yellow earth, one lone girl wears red. In this vast and boundless frame, all this heavy yellow encircles this red; it's a kind of restraining of human passion and illustrates that many things are immutable and frozen, that the individual is powerless. *Red Sorghum* is different; the color red is displayed to the fullest extent here. Simply speaking, its theme is just the praising of life. As long as

the plot, events, and characters all made sense together, we utilized red to
the fullest, allowing it to really penetrate these points.

Did you handle the sound in any particular way?
We intentionally made several sections of music very loud. The *suona* horn
is inherently very loud, and we had thirty *suona* all play clamorously together. This is how we wanted to display the sound. The singing of these
songs was actually influenced by traditional northern opera. Opera has a
longer tradition than popular songs; its national culture runs much deeper.
From my experiences living in the countryside, peasants have spent more
time with opera than with popular song. Northern opera has a fundamental
roughness, an openness. It's bold and unrestrained and is often sung over
the empty countryside. Peasants all over the world sing loudly and don't use
that kind of refined, controlled, or low voice; rather, they shout, wail, and
sing to entertain themselves. So we integrated the particular qualities of
opera in composing the music, but we didn't reveal its concrete time or
place—as long as it was the northern countryside, it was OK. It wasn't like
Yellow Earth's concrete explanation of northern Shaanxi province.

    We blended together operas from the provinces of Shaanxi, Henan, Shan-
dong, and Shanxi, remolded them, spoke with a mixed accent, both resembling and not resembling them. We did all this intentionally. As far as I was
concerned, as long as they opened their throats like peasants and yelled as
loud as possible when singing, aggressive and disorderly shouting was just
fine with me.

    The actor's lines were the same. They all shouted what could be shouted,
yelling from beginning to end in very loud voices. Only the asides took on a
contrasting method, utilizing the most common and calm of voices to tell
us—almost without any feeling—about my grandpa and grandma. When
you hear his voice, it's completely numb. Jiang Wen dubbed it himself.

    With this calm intonation of a modern person, it seems as if he's already
told the story a thousand times. There's no feeling of liveliness. We also consciously utilized this kind of calm and ordinary intonation to form a contrast
against the film. Here lies the so-called modern consciousness. The film is a
story of long ago, and the characters of the story are all full of a vitality of
life; the sound, action, and events are all intense. The modern narrator simply doesn't have this much passion. When this performer dubbed the film,
we didn't show him the picture, had him read in a dark room, and didn't let

him memorize his lines. If he'd said it from memory, then it would have carried the smell of performance. We wanted it to be like reading a book aloud.

Is this to illustrate that modern people don't have as much vitality of life as those before?
It's to suggest that Chinese people today have lost some of this passion for life. Living and spiritual conditions no longer have that earlier kind of rich vitality. To take it a step further, if a nation wants to develop toward the future, if it wants to be powerful and prosperous or influential, it simply has to have a vitality and burning passion toward life. No matter how much you suffer and no matter how tragic your fate, you need courage to live. This courage can't be worn away; otherwise, humanity would have no way of moving forward or developing toward the future. I think that several thousand years of humanity have also relied upon this kind of courage—an unceasing desire and vitality toward controlling one's own destiny. Every person hopes that his or her life will get better and better; this idea underlies everything. This is a critique of the modern mentality of Chinese people. Even though a country may be poor—its people poverty-stricken with all kinds of problems and much suffering—if people want to live, they should live to their hearts content, and they should have spiritual passion. So we used the counterpoint of the aside to convey a veiled meaning. We didn't want to be too obvious. It was enough if we conveyed this meaning.

Also, I feel it's really quite interesting when the grandson talks about his grandpa. On the mainland, when someone is called "grandson," it means that he's a coward or weak in character. The grandson talks about his grandpa, but doesn't do it well. If you live like this then you're the grandson, and you'll never be the grandpa. It's pretty interesting.

In Mo Yan's novel, the measure of the female protagonist's morality . . .
That she didn't sleep with only one person?

You changed it so that she only has one lover. Does this have anything to do with the issue of morality?
No. Whether the novel reads that "my grandpa" did or didn't "enter into my grandma's *kang* [bed]," I'm not sure even if he did, what would be the difference? My grandma dared to do anything, as long as she willed it. Mo

Yan describes my grandma as sexually unconventional, yet there's no incident of this in the novel. But he always writes. . . . Once we'd pulled together the structure, we'd already decided how the characters had to be, and the events were already simplified. Other than the fighting of nine years later, the section about nine years earlier occupies two thirds of the film's length, which was concentrated into events completed in six or seven days—the time around the marriage ceremony, returning home after three days, being kidnapped by bandits, after which they made wine, and it was finished! The original novel depicts many events over a certain number of years, and it's very easy to fall in love with many different men over this time. It was hard for us to imagine that over the length of several days, a woman would be able to sleep with other men after ardently loving one man this much. I don't think this is a question of unconventionality; rather, her falling in love with several men would cause her passionate love to become suspect. Over these few days, her love with this man should be the top priority. It would definitely be interesting if I were to revise the time structure and depict the events of three years in the sorghum fields. While this woman is loose—and this looseness is great—I feel that there's no need to think of this in terms of traditional morality. Characters have to go along with the structure of the film. You can't force an unsuitable structure just to depict how anti-traditional, unconventional, and unrestrained she might be. Otherwise, your ideas will be too obvious and could cause people to feel uncomfortable. You can imagine the flaming passion of a man and woman over five or six days; they'd probably have no time to even think about the possibility of sleeping with someone else!

The structure of the novel is extremely complicated, with juxtapositions of time and space. The film also simplified them.
The flashbacks in the film don't follow the events of the novel that closely. I felt that this method wouldn't be new and worried that it would be too formalistic. I wasn't very interested in this. If the methodology is too strong, the imagery too distinctive, or ideas laid bare too obviously, then you've produced nothing more than counterpoint and contrast, which will cause your film and what you've said to seem artificial and affected. We told it in a simple, straightforward way, with the overall structure maintaining a kind of naturalness and easy sense of narration.

According to Tian Zhuangzhuang, you all were influenced by Neo-Realism and the French New Wave in the course of your studies.

Good films have had influence on us. To say that they haven't is to talk nonsense. No one lives in a vacuum. I believe that the world's great masters, geniuses, and super-genius have always been the products of their times, that they've been influenced by the overall creative atmosphere of their times. Regardless of whether they want to be like other people or not, they've all been influenced. But as we conceived *Red Sorghum*, we didn't refer to any other films, but much rather hoped to make it according to our own ideas and not think about other films as much as possible. In this way we could avoid directly making reference to other films. The quality of a film should lie in its internal and inner influences as opposed to its external form, and its structure should unconsciously rely on these internal things. No one is so stupid as to directly imitate a film and directly copy someone else's success. This tells everyone that you have no creative ability, that you're an idiot. Even if you succeed, you're still an idiot. The essence of art is creativity. The influence from foreign films is in terms of thought, in terms of ways of thinking. Directors like Federico Fellini, Jean-Luc Godard, and Michelangelo Antonioni have helped us to understand that it doesn't actually matter how a film is filmed, so long as you convey your own ideas. Yet I don't want to be like Chinese films of the past, invariable and frozen, with only one kind of fixed pattern of thinking.

When you were at the film academy did you often discuss film with your classmates?

Public discussions were never very interesting. Everyone spoke extremely politely, and everyone was afraid of making public fools of themselves. Everything said in public was well thought out. It was more interesting in private, since people were a bit more open and would comment a lot. If a film was good, they'd say it was good, and if it was bad, they'd criticize it. We were full of rebelliousness then, wanting to make films in the future that were different from others. When we filmed *One and Eight*, the four of us—including Zhang Junzhao and me—made a pact, spelling out what we would do if we didn't make it well. When *Red Sorghum* was filmed, I also gave Wu Tianming three guarantees—no trouble from the government, artistic quality, and commercial box-office success.

So is Red Sorghum *drawing large audiences?*
It is really making money. In the first round of showings in Beijing, Shandong, and Fuzhou, tickets were all completely sold out and scalped tickets were going for five to ten ygan each—normally one ticket costs three mao. I think it's great that this many people like to see it.

How have older film circles regarded Red Sorghum?
These elders of the film world haven't liked it. *Yellow Earth, Old Well,* and *Red Sorghum* have won awards overseas, yet some people ask why we should want to go to capitalist countries to attend film exhibitions. Some people wrote letters criticizing Wu Tianming's *Old Well* as having "sold out our own mothers"—that it exposed our negative aspects, our poverty and ignorance, and that foreigners only liked it for its novelty. So I'm very grateful to Wu Tianming; he's allowed me to film without any apprehensions. When these people criticize us, it's caused us to feel even more rebellious. We simply have to show them. In school in the past we often said that someday when we made a film, we wouldn't be like others. Chinese people are too inhibited; everything in this society is about politics and society. People aren't people; they're stature is already small, and then they shrink back even further. So we definitely wanted to restore human feelings and relationships. China's five thousand years of history and three thousand years of feudalism are a very heavy burden. So I wanted to make *Red Sorghum.* I believe that Chinese people have already changed a lot. The stifling of politics has been around for too long, and they'll surely want to rise up. I'm not interested in politics. Art dies because of freedom and lives because of oppression. So China is now boiling over and is really seething with excitement. Deng Xiaoping opened the door, and people poked their heads out to look—oh, so this is what the world is like. Once you've opened the door, you can't go back. Although there have been political movements—anti-capitalist liberalism, anti-spiritual pollution—they're all transitory. In the future, China will definitely produce even better directors and works.

A Donkey, a PropeRer, and Young Sorghum

At the end of April, while I was still filming *Old Well,* I pooled some money together and first went to Shandong to look and find out where the sorghum might be in Shandong nowadays. Peasants have all switched to growing other, more valuable cash crops—things like peanuts. I first chose a piece of land according to its terrain—about sixteen acres of land over which hills undulated nicely—and then looked for some peasants with whom I could negotiate. Over thirty households came. Nowadays, peasants can be very troublesome; they just want money. As soon as I saw the worn out land, I immediately knew that nothing had grown on it for many years, but they said it was valuable. Then I told them, you'll make money, but it also has to be acceptable to us—you can't ask for too much. Eventually, I gave them the money and was relieved when I saw the seedlings sprout. I didn't go back to check on it.

In June, I brought the whole production team to Shandong and was dumbfounded when I saw the sorghum. How could it have grown only to the height of chives? It couldn't even hide your knees, and sorghum should be as high as a roof. These peasants thought that since it was only for a film, there was no need to take care of it after the seeds were planted; they didn't even spread fertilizer or water it. Sorghum needs a lot of water. Every time it's watered, it'll grow a bit less than an inch. So our whole production team watered it. We were first peasants for half a month. I was very worried because the location team was spending night and day in the fields and costing me over a thousand *yqan* per day. We got water from wells and bought fertilizer. We had a fire truck come, too. We grabbed the hose like this and sprayed water over the sorghum. We fired guns for rain every day. Heaven really helped us when it began to rain after a while.

These activities lasted twenty days when one big rain caused the stalks of sorghum to grow like children, every joint making crisp sounds. We were really happy about these big stalks, but there was still a problem. Having thoroughly discussed growing a pure breed of sorghum, these peasants had grown half a field of hybrid sorghum for us. I was dumbfounded—of about sixteen acres, eight had only grown this tall. [He brings his hand to his shoulder.] There's no way it could have hidden anyone's head.

Moreover, hybrid sorghum isn't very appealing to look at. Its stalks are really sturdy, thick, and short, and its ears are just a lump like this—not very appealing. It's not like pure sorghum, which is so tall, with a soft top and its ears spreading out. It's beautiful when the wind blows. But what could I do? I had no choice but to film only those eight acres. So it seems that I really did all I could to make even this kind of film, and the result wasn't too bad, ha ha ha. . . . Think about it, if I'd been given a hundred and sixty acres of sorghum to film, I could have displayed it over a wide screen, which would definitely have been more appealing than now.

Also, Mo Yan's description is very supernatural—"Blood-like sorghum," he writes. That sorghum is just this color. [He points to a light brown-colored doll on the floor.] If you looked down from a mountain to a hundred and sixty-acre expanse of land, it could be a sheet of red. I now only had eight acres. What was the use of it? When the ears open, the stalks all dry up as yellow as maize. If a person were to direct a close up shot toward it, the background would be full of dried up leaves, and where would be the ears of sorghum?

We filmed when it was green. It wasn't red sorghum; we couldn't wait until its ears opened because it would look bad. We called that green a sprightly green to indicate young sorghum. You should always film her when she is a young girl and shouldn't wait until she's an old woman, right? So making this film was really interesting. Even up to today no one has noticed that we only filmed the sorghum within a short period of its life. There are only twenty days from green to red, so we had to scramble to film it. If Chen Kaige had filmed it, he'd want it to be profound and deep and would never be able to finish it in time.

That donkey was also a lot of fun. Our female protagonist is really beautiful, yet whenever the donkey saw her he'd throw her off; he did this to her so many times. When we'd hit him, he'd walk in circles with this female performer pulling at him from above, saying . . . [he laughs] . . . she said that the property man should take responsibility for the donkey. I then suggested that he find a gentler, smaller one. He said that it wouldn't be right for the film, but I told him that no one would notice the donkey. In the end, he found a donkey this short—you get on his back and your feet touch the ground. At the beginning of the scene, people hid in the sorghum and prodded him with sticks. The donkey just took a few steps and we scrambled to film them. The female performer asked how she was to act. I said why don't you just walk from here to there. This is how we filmed this scene, and the result wasn't too bad. Later, some people even said that it was very artistic. Ha ha!

We only had a budget of seventy thousand *renminbi*. If we'd had twice the money, we could have used six helicopters. We needed the wind to blow now, so what were we to do? We brought in a propeller, put it on a truck, and had it blow wind. That wind was so strong that the first five rows of sorghum were all blown to the ground. Those tall stalks became so crooked and ugly. The last twenty rows stood over there not moving at all, so we could only choose from the middle section where the sorghum was swaying fairly calmly.

As for making sorghum wine, everything has modernized now, so who knows how they made sorghum wine fifty years ago? Mo Yan didn't know either, so we blindly worked it out. There's also the earlier sedan chair scene. I asked Mo Yan how the sedan bearers jolted the chair, and he said he didn't know either. So I made it up myself. And the song—I wrote all the lines of the song they sang while jolting her chair. After seeing it, many people said that it preserved folk customs very well. What folk customs? I made it all up. Even that battle scene was also filmed in a rush. We didn't know what we were shooting.

Asking the Questions: Interview with Zhang Yimou

MICHEL CIMENT/1992

You have often declared that your films were inspired by an image. Is this also true of The Story of Qiu Ju?

As always, I started from a novel, but this time I wanted to do something different. I wanted to change styles and, in the beginning, I concentrated more on the narrative than on images. After reading the novel, which I liked a lot, I tried to find the best way of adapting it for the screen and realized that the camera should be at eye level, that it should actually be a character, among the others. Therefore, almost half of the film was shot with a hidden camera to obtain the maximum effect of spontaneity. To prevent actors' awareness, the best solution would have been to film from a high angle, but I decided against it. The camera had to be at the same level with the actors. This was very difficult because the amateurs' tendency is to look into the lens. The first sequence of the film represents well the type of atmosphere I wanted to create. People walk, move forward and little by little the viewer sees Qiu Ju. I wanted to tell a simple, normal story about simple, normal people in a straightforward manner.

Did you choose your two cinematographers, Chi Xiaoning and Yu Xiaoqun, according to this new shooting method?

In fact, there is a third one, Liu Hong Yi, who is not credited. I needed more cinematographers because I had several cameras. I also wanted people with

From Positif #382 (September 1992). Reprinted by permission. Translated by Lenute Giukin.

experience in documentaries. Chi Xiaoning had worked previously on several advertising films.

You give a lot of attention to colors and, as it often happens, the dominant is red found in red peppers, the corn, and in Qiu Ju's red clothes.
I did not choose colors deliberately as in the past. I shot in the north of China where red is a dominant color. On the other hand, the film was realized in the two months before and two months after the New Year, this January and February. During this period, red is used a lot more for holidays. It was consequently very realistic. The people from this northern culture, called the culture of the Yellow River, like very strong colors for reasons I don't know and ignore.

What appealed to you in the novel of Chen Yuanbin, and how did you work with Liu Heng, your scriptwriter?
Chen Yuanbin is a young writer who has published before, but this novel is his first true novel and obtained the prize of the best Chinese fiction this year. What I like the most is the naturalness, the fluidity of the style characteristic of a (real) born storyteller. The literary critics think that with this novel a new writing style was born in China. As I also wanted to radically change my approach, it seemed to me that this novel was particularly well-suited. The first change made with Liu Heng was to move the action from the South to the North (the novel takes place in the region of Anhui). I thought that to really succeed in this kind of film, I had to know the surroundings very well. Therefore, I set it in the region where I was born and grew up. Because I am familiar with it, I could establish real relations with the people whose dialect I know. The problem was not just to tell a story but to know how characters move, eat, or talk. It had to be very precise. I worked very well with Liu Heng. He wrote the first adaptation after I changed a couple of things, and finally he elaborated a third version of the script. We had a similar collaboration on *Ju Dou.*

The title of the novel, Wanjia susong, *is different than the movie's title,* Qiu Ju da guansi.
The novel's title means "the family takes legal action" and is very literary, while the movie's title belongs to the spoken language and literally means "Qiu Ju makes a complaint." This also emphasizes the woman's character

whose first name is very common in the northern plains of China. In the
novel her name is Qiu He Ping.

*During the Cultural Revolution, you were forced to work in the countryside for three
years. To what extent did this occupation allow you, the son of a doctor, to get
acquainted with the peasant world?*
I learned a lot during this period. I planted seeds, cut tree branches, harvested
crops, changed the products of land in food, and learned to cook. I also took
care of cows, horses, and donkeys. In this movie, there are lots of things that
were part of my past experience in the countryside. In fact, I was sent to a
place very close to the one where I shot the film, about an hour away.

*Are you Qiu Ju insofar as you were not allowed into the film school because you
passed the age limit and for a long time fought until you had to appeal to the
Minister of Culture in order to obtain justice, considering that your studies were
postponed because of the Cultural Revolution?*
It is not important to know if I am Qiu Ju or if her story reminds me of my
own because this story is very ordinary and happens often in China. One
does not know who to address, what to do, or where to go. At the beginning,
most problems are not important, but they become so because of the bureaucratic system and the difficulties one has to live through. I wanted to represent this common situation with humor. Before coming to Venice, I was
asked this question in my country. I answered that what Qiu Ju wanted is a
word she uses in the film *shuafa*, a Chinese word which does not refer to an
excuse, but to an answer, an explanation or clarification. With *Ju Dou* and
Raise the Red Lantern, I had the same experience. The films were never distributed and no one ever gave a *shuafa* about the banning. It is the same thing
in the novel and the movie: the lawyer helped her a lot, worked for her, and
in the end managed to put the head of the village in prison, but no one
bothered to know exactly what Qiu Ju wanted.

*She does not react to what the letter-writer/village scribe tells her, even though he
announces the conclusion of the story by informing her that he succeeded in send-
ing/condemning to death a certain number of people.*
In China, this character is very common because a lot of people are still
illiterate. But there is also a lot of black humor in this scene. In the end,

when the head of the village is imprisoned, the public dies of laughter because the scene with the village scribe is interpreted as an ill omen.

The movie shows that the idea of justice is relative because the nature of a judgment changes in time; Qiu Ju does not have the same relations with the head of the village after her delivery. The absolute justice, is it impossible?
There is a gap between the familial justice she demands, the village being a big family, and the justice of the court. She simply wanted to be better treated by the head of the village, and, in the end, he is arrested and taken away by the administrative machine [which is] carried away in the wrong direction. The comedy comes from the discrepancy between the two situations. One has to understand that this type of Chinese village, as I already mentioned, is like a big family. Qiu Ju wanted justice at a particular moment; later she has nothing to do with it.

Do you mean that the authorities dispense justice, but the individual also has to fight; otherwise, he will never obtain anything?
Yes. If you do not ask questions, no one will ever give you an answer. One has to fight to make things happen. In China, in order to solve the most insignificant problem, one has to try twenty times and spend years on it. Among the officials, no one really makes errors, but in the last analysis, there is no answer. Making claims is the beginning of a democracy. In this movie I wanted to say that every Chinese person—not only the peasant—has to do the same thing: fight to win the case and discover oneself in the battle to achieve his or her goal.

Even if he regrets in the end, like Qiu Ju, to have undertaken it?
It is true that she is unhappy in the end, but it is only because she did not obtain what she wanted: an explanation. The meaning of the last shot—a frozen image—is to meditate on what the law can really bring to people. Is this justice: if someone causes you harm, do you have to return it? Is this really an answer?

How many professional actors play in the film, and how did you integrate the amateurs?
Gong Li and those playing the husband, the police officer, and the head of the village were professional actors. They had to live in the village for two

months before we started shooting in order to get acquainted with the people, learn their dialect, read the same things, dress like them. It was the best way to integrate them: making them share the daily lives of the villagers. The village people had never seen a camera or a microphone before and this was a problem. I decided to familiarize them with this equipment by trailing it under their eyes for a few weeks. It was necessary because not all the sequences were shot with the hidden camera. As I could not ask the local people to put on an act, I asked the professional actors to behave like peasants. They had to compromise, and by inversing roles, I had all freedom to work. For rehearsals, I eliminated projectors using at the maximum the natural light and reduced the technical team to a minimum.

Did you have to repeat the shots often because of the numerous non-professionals?
Indeed, I had to shoot a lot of film. Out of ten takes, maybe one was good. It happened that for one single shot, we had to work a whole evening, the next day, and a part of the day after. For the scenes shot with a hidden camera, we installed a wooden board in the street for five or six days. The day before shooting, the cinematographer set up his camera behind it. All night and the next morning, he had to stay behind it without moving, without even going to the bathroom, until noon when the street animation was at its peak. Through a hole, he observed what was happening. We would then suddenly remove the board and he filmed the scene. Of course, sometimes a person would look into the camera and we had to make new arrangements and start all over again in a different place!

Did the fact that you shot a lot of film make the editing longer?
Not really because I edited the film during the shooting. I like to work in this way. I shoot during the day and edit until three in the morning.

The character of Meizi, Qiu Ju's sister-in-law emphasizes, through her surprise, Qiu Ju's energy and determination. Considering that she is not a professional actress, in what ways was this experience new for her?
It was the first time that she went to a city. She lived in that village and never had enough money to make the trip. Indeed, from a narrative point of view, she calls attention to Qiu Ju's strength. Because Qiu Ju is pregnant, she needs to go with somebody. There is a logical reason for her presence. Additionally,

her silence shows the surprise she feels at her sister-in-law's behavior but is also characteristic to the countryside people who speak little.

This film is a co-production of China and Hong Kong. The previous film was produced in Taiwan by Hou Hsiao-Hsien. How are these productions put together by different Chinese companies?
I do not pay attention to these financial collaborations and ignore [what is] the role of each producer. I receive a salary and this is all.

Why did you choose, for the first time, a contemporary subject?
The same reason I mentioned in the beginning. I wanted to go into a new direction, to adopt a different style. The most obvious transformation was to choose a contemporary subject considering that all my other films take place in the past.

You were an actor in the film of Wu Tianming, Old Well. *How did this experience help you in your work with actors?*
It was important for me to be an actor before directing because only if one was an actor can one understand the importance of this work. It also helps me direct my actors and know what they feel. In China when we shoot, the actors sometimes do not feel comfortable because of a lack of organization on the sets. Having gone through this myself allowed me to make up for what they lack and to improve their performances through editing or better organization. I think that in a film the most important element is the actor; everything should contribute to enhancing his or her performance—from music and photography to editing. The whole team has to be at their service because in the end it is through them that the film communicates with the public. There are several ways of shooting a film, different styles that might age in time, but what makes a movie last or not is the actors' performances. Only the actor allows us to know the human being.

Your education prepared you to be a cinematographer and no visual aspects were unknown to you. Acting gave you access to another dimension in film: life and characters.
Of course, being a cinematographer was important in my formation as a director, but having to perform was for me the decisive experience. The cinematographer also depends on the actor and not the opposite. This is why,

now that I am a director, I like to collaborate with my cinematographer—to speed up his work and prevent delaying the actors. I use my past experience to eliminate the gaps between shots, which spoil the actor's performance. Being an actor and a cinematographer myself helps me create a pleasant atmosphere, thanks to a shooting without slack periods.

You also played with Gong Li in A Terracota Warrior *by Ching Siu Tung. Could you talk a little about your work with your fetish actress?*
I played with her shortly before directing *Ju Dou*, and she was the main character in four of my films. I work with her as with all my actors. I like to start one month before the shooting and discuss the script in detail with them, so they can ask questions and also make suggestions. I like to listen to what they have to say. During these weeks of preparation, they wear their character's clothes to get accustomed to them and have their hair done as during the shooting. This way they become more familiar with the characters. Around ten days before the first shots, we begin the rehearsals where I record on tapes that they watch later. Once the shooting starts, I keep the script and do not discuss it with them again, unless it has to do with important and complex scenes that can be debated the evening before the shooting. At the end of the day, I want them to relax and meet each other because I do not want to impose on them too much of my point of view. There are two types of actors: the cerebral actor who meditates a lot before playing a role and prepares every scene in detail, and the emotional one who steps into his character and plays instinctively. Gong Li belongs to this category. Once she prepares with me and I explain to her clearly what I want, I let her follow her instincts.

Despite the fact that the four movies are very different, the female character is often strong and takes her destiny in her own hands.
Today in China men and women have more egalitarian relations, but medieval thinking governed my country for thousands of years, and men always had a dominant position. This remains inscribed in the spirit of people, especially in the countryside. My movies are all adapted from novels that have as central characters a strong female figure, and from the narrative perspective this is necessary to establish a contrast with the feudal mentality. On the other hand, as I am faithful to the novels I adapt . . .

But you decided to choose these novels!
The best way to draw attention to a character is to place them in a difficult situation and a complex social milieu. The external pressure highlights his or her personality, which has to be strong in order to control their destiny. The new Chinese literature that concentrates on oppressive contexts uses this approach. Female characters are in an inferior social position but are more intelligent and sensitive than men. They are particularly capable of touching the public. It is also important and new for the Chinese viewers to see in action a strong woman. It is a recent phenomenon in Chinese culture.

In your films there is also a superior authority, the husband in Ju Dou, *the master we rarely see in* Raise the Red Lantern *and in* The Story of Qiu Ju, *the judicial power.*
I was always interested in the relation between a fragile personality, [who is] nonetheless strong, and a powerful force exerted in these three films. The Chinese woman had always to submit to the others' orders. Very few did not obey. But nowadays there are more women who have the courage to oppose the established authority. It is appropriate to show this in a moment where women become aware of it.

Su Tong, the novelist of Raise the Red Lantern, *does he belong to the same genera-tion as the author of* The Story of Qiu Ju?
All the writers I adapted are about the same age. The author of *Red Sorghum* was thirty-two when he wrote his novel, *Ju Dou*'s author was thirty-four, Su Tong twenty-eight, and Chen Yuanbin thirty-six. They are a new generation, different from the previous ones through their style and themes. They ana-lyze society from a modern angle, even if they talk about the past. They abandoned the propaganda to adopt a new human point of view that ob-serves society from inside. They all started in the eighties.

Do they like the cinema?
They are very flexible culturally. They have a particular interest in cinema and participate in panels on film. Every time I finish a movie, I organize a screening where the writer is invited to talk in public. We, the Chinese direc-tors, have very close relations with the new writers. They are even my friends and always help me a lot. I think that cinema also influenced their literary creation. Additionally, the adaptation of their novels to the screen made

them known to a larger public, not only in China, but in Taiwan, Hong Kong, Japan, and in the West. This is stimulating for an artist. It is also amusing because these movies being very successful abroad; the novelists are as enthusiastic to see their novels adapted to the screen as the directors are to acquire the rights of a new good novel.

When were Ju Dou *and* Raise the Red Lantern *authorized in China?*
Ju Dou is right now in theaters, and *Raise the Red Lantern* will come out in October. I think that both movies will be very successful, considering that two hundred copies were made of each of them, which is pretty unusual; *Red Sorghum* had only one hundred copies. There was a premiere of *Ju Dou* in Shanghai with Gong Li's participation in the presence of a few thousand viewers restrained by fifty policemen. The curiosity was stirred up by the nomination of the Oscar in Hollywood, the success abroad, and the long banning of the film. It is always like this in China: if you tell people they cannot see something, they want to see it even more.

How do you explain the change in attitude of authorities?
No one really explained it to me. In China, especially for the co-productions with Hong Kong or a foreign country in general, the procedure is the following: you submit the script for approval to the censors, and when the movie is finished you have to send it again to obtain their approval. *Ju Dou's* script was authorized, but the censors thought the film was different without specifying in what way. It was the same case with *The Story of Qiu Ju.* I think their release has to do a lot with Deng Xiaoping's recent discourse which relaxed the atmosphere in China. Nevertheless, none of the members of the censorship committee wanted to take the responsibility of giving an explanation. I think that the distribution office simply submitted a request document to release the two films and the committee stamped it without any other procedure. It was just a formal act. It had to wait. This explains why *The Story of Qiu Ju* makes Chinese laugh so much: everyone went through this experience. This was at least the audience's reaction at the Chinese film festival where it won the Grand Prize and also in previews and press presentations. Nearly two hundred copies will be distributed in October.

What relations do you have with Chinese filmmakers from Taiwan like Hou Hsiao-Hsien and Edward Yang, and do you see any differences in your film approaches?

The first time I met them was in Hong Kong in 1985. There I discovered their movies and liked them immediately. I also found out that they liked *Yellow Earth* by Chen Kaige very much. We have close relations despite the fact that we do not see each other often, sometimes for more than a year. In general we meet at festivals. Seeing each others' movies is a discovery because we did not know for a long time what was shown on screens. I don't think [though] there are many reciprocal influences, and when we meet it is more like a friends' reunion than a directors' discussion. But, of course, everyone wants to know what the others have done.

Taiwanese films treat more contemporary subjects, using fewer metaphors (excepting *The Story of Qiu Ju*, of course) than Chinese movies, and stylistically use more long takes and deep focus.

The movies from continental China are influenced by the literary tradition that creates stories from a historical and metaphorical perspective. Therefore, our films are usually situated in the past. Taiwan is relatively a new country with less history. Their style is linked to the Japanese cinema. They were occupied by Japan for fifty years and the Japanese presence influenced their thinking. Our cinema was under two influences: first, the traditional Chinese artistic and literary creation and secondly, the Western film. I would have difficulties pointing out specific influences, but my generation, which studied between 1979 and 1982, was widely exposed to the New Wave and the Italian neo-realism. Also, to American cinema. But when we left school and went to the countryside, in the most representative places of our culture, we tried to find authentic sources of inspiration, keeping in mind the Western film images we had seen in school.

Zhang Yimou's Black Comedy: *The Story of Qiu Ju*

L A W   W A I - M I N G / 1 9 9 2

O N   H I S   W A Y   T O   Venice with *Qiu Ju*, Zhang Yimou spent two days in Hong Kong just as the film was being shown here. Thus, he was bound—under the special arrangements of the film company—to manage to find the time to spend a day publicizing it, accepting interviews with various media representatives, one after another. *City Entertainment* was invited but was only granted the half-hour interview allotted to everyone. Simply touching on a few subjects only suits casual conversation and chatting about recent events is an inadequate substitute for a thorough interview in which the director addresses his personal style and concerns. Once our time was up, Zhang Yimou even commented, "We've only just begun to talk." We truly were unable to enjoy enough conversation.

When I talked with Zhang Yimou, I couldn't have addressed everything I wanted in a day and night of conversation because these still-called "Fifth Generation" new Chinese directors have a self-awareness unparalleled by their predecessors; they maturely consider both social circumstances and artistic style, and, most importantly, express themselves articulately. Their works have always gotten to the very heart of issues and, along with other media, have contributed to the construction of modernization in China.

Looking at Chinese cinema of Hong Kong, China, and Taiwan today, the films of Taiwan's Hou Hsiao-Hsien and Edward Yang are the most rich and profound because they are able to address any subject matter with few politi-

From *City Entertainment: Film Biweekly* No. 351 (17 September 1992). Reprinted by permission. Translated by Stephanie Deboer.

cal misgivings. In comparison, directors such as Chen Kaige, Zhang Yimou, Tian Zhuangzhuang, and Huang Jianxin seem rather narrow. Yet consideration of their environment as well as recognition of their efforts within their narrow confines has garnered people's respect. At the time of this interview, in fact, although the ban on Zhang Yimou's work had been lifted, Tian Zhaungzhuang's new work was encountering problems. Seeing this, one begins to appreciate how difficult it can be to make one's way through this world. So I began by asking:

Have all your current films been allowed for showing in mainland China?
Yes. They're being shown now.

Are they being shown together?
No, it depends upon the decision of each province or city.

How has the reaction to them been?
Generally, pretty good. *Red Sorghum* sold over one hundred prints; *Ju Dou* has now sold over two hundred. People are probably curious—generally speaking, when a film has been suppressed for a long time, the appetite for it actually increases.

Other than distribution sales, what has been the public reaction to your films?
I haven't heard yet. They've probably only recently been shown; Shanghai has just begun to show *Ju Dou*.

How is the situation in mainland China? The ban on your film has been lifted, yet it seems that problems have also emerged with Tian Zhaungzhuang's new work.
Since Deng Xiaoping's southern tour, the entire situation has taken a turn for the better.[1] But this has only just begun—we haven't yet seen how significant the change will be. I'm sure you know that conditions on the mainland always change slowly. The lifting of the ban on *Ju Dou* has been regarded by some in China as a sign of opening up. No one has said that Tian Zhuangzhuang's film won't ever be approved. It's just that because its subject is sensitive, no higher-ups have publicly defined their position toward it.

Those of us overseas don't understand the actual situation in China very well. In the past, some works were banned and then quickly had the ban lifted. Was this

because two factions were struggling against each another, and doesn't what we're seeing now also reflect this pattern?
That isn't necessarily the situation now. It's just that everyone is waiting for the Fourteenth Party Congress; only after this Congress has convened will things be clear. I think the problem with Tian Zhuangzhuang's film is also related to this. First shelve it for a while and wait until things can be seen more clearly. We're all used to this process. *One and Eight* also went through this—once it was put aside for two years, there was no longer any problem. *Ju Dou* was also put aside for a few years.

It seems to me that your filming methods have changed in your recent films. Have you been aware of this?
I've been quite conscious of it. When I began making films, I tended to construct and control. I was from that school of filmmaking, and I liked rather intense things. So early on, I created very powerful images; I'm quite good at this. This could be regarded as a kind of style, although people may have different opinions about it. I feel—and the responsibility lies with myself— that I'm not very good at narrative. So I've changed my methods to see if I could make up for such shortcomings. But actually, every film contains aspects of this early approach—its use just depends upon whether or not it's appropriate or achieves the look you want.

I could use structuralism to look at your works because beginning from Red Sorghum *up to* Ju Dou, *the plots all develop through repeated changes.*
I don't know about structuralism, but the changes began from *Ju Dou*, although it might not have been very obvious. I'm only looking back at myself. I think every director looks back at him- or herself, looks at what was inadequate in the past. When I made *Ju Dou*, everyone felt that it was very dangerous because I hadn't made that kind of film before. I'd never filmed anything very realistic or pedestrian. I'd previously only made intense, heavily dramatic films. So when I decided to make this one, my assistants all had real doubts. Then I decided to go to another extreme to handle the subject of this film. Since it was to be realistic, I could make it even more realistic by using things like concealed cameras—make it as realistic as possible. As a result, the distance from the past was great.

Red Sorghum *and* Ju Dou *were on the whole rather evenly controlled and don't resemble the extreme appearance of earlier films.*

I've probably matured. I actually feel that *Red Sorghum* is good at some points and bad at others. Some places were brilliant, other places I didn't know how to handle, and the whole effect was very rough. *Red Sorghum*'s strength is its kind of primeval power, but as I've continued to make films, my filmmaking has become more strictly controlled. Generally speaking, the more films you make the better your sense of balance. Film is something you or anyone else can make. It all lies in an accurate sense of balance. The master or apprentice is determined by this. It all depends upon how you make it. I think Hou Hsiao-Hsien's sense of balance is very good. But it's difficult to say how it's captured because there are many ways of achieving it.

To ask a question our readers like to ask, I'd like to address your view of women and the color red because these are the most striking aspects of all your films.
I really like the color red. It probably has something to do with my childhood hometown. Ever since I began to like art, I've felt that red is the color loved by the entire Yellow River basin—it's displayed in every aspect of daily life in rural areas. The essential expression of folk art is found in those memorial ceremonies, all of which feature red. I also like red because I like intense things, and the use of it creates a vivid scene rather quickly. As for *Qiu Ju*, there really are that many red peppers in the countryside, but now I feel that there were too many of them in the film. Looking back, I think that reducing them by half would have made it even more natural.

As for women, the protagonists of my few films have all been women, and I've been made into a feminist director. What is most significant, I think, is that Chinese literature emphasizes female protagonists. What it's most adept at depicting is primarily women. Yet they're all written by men. Mo Yan, Su Tong—they're all good at writing about women. When we select them, we mainly consider two aspects: On the one hand is choosing roles for Gong Li, for this actress; on the other hand is the fact that women in Chinese literature are a bit more complex than men. Writers all know that placing a figure in a complex environment full of obstacles makes depicting a plot relatively easy. In the countryside, the patriarchal situation is very grave; therefore, if the actress was replaced by a man, then there'd be no *Qiu Ju*.

When I originally chose the novel, *The Wan Family Lawsuit*, I was struck by its brand of black humor. What's interesting about the film is that it doesn't have any truly good or bad people. It isn't about the problems of bureaucracy but is rather about the problems of ordinary rural people. China is still an agricultural society and has a total rural population of .6 billion. China can by no means be solely represented by Shenzhen or Shanghai. If China truly is to become more free, democratic, or modernized, this is only possible once the .6 billion-strong rural population improves its awareness and directly participates. Therefore, if you want them to awake to a sense of respect for the individual, you must understand all this.

Chinese society, no matter how metaphysical the philosophy, all relates itself to the family. Thus, a country appealing to its people to pledge their loyalty can easily say that you are a son of the nation and that the party is your mother. The problem of the countryside is that they tend to look at problems in terms of family ethics.

Throughout China's modernization, intellectuals all know how shortcomings in China's national character have caused various doctrines to falter in China. *Qiu Ju* is also aimed at this type of basic issue. Yet I feel that this film avoids the largest obstacle to modernization—that of bureaucracy.

I don't feel that it avoids involvement in anything; it's simply a matter of choosing what you're going to deal with. Bureaucratism isn't such a big problem nowadays. What I feel is significant about this story is that there's no obstacle to each link. If an obstacle—say, a bad person—had appeared, that would have become the focus of attention. Placing the blame on him or her would have simplified the story. If there's going to be a bureaucrat, then everyone at least hopes for an honest one. If there's a just official, then it seems that any problem can be solved and everything will be fine.

Becoming a Part of Life: An Interview with Zhang Yimou

ROBERT SKLAR/1993

IN THE PAST HALF decade, Zhang Yimou has become China's internationally most famous filmmaker, but to make that simple observation only reveals the visible (to non-Chinese) tip of the hidden iceberg where politics and culture meet in contemporary China. His first film as a director, *Red Sorghum* (1988), was immensely popular in China as well as top prize winner at the 1988 Berlin Film Festival. However, later works that were acclaimed overseas, *Ju Dou* (1990) and *Raise the Red Lantern* (1991), had been banned in China by hard-line bureaucrats who dominated Chinese film culture following the 1989 Beijing massacres. Zhang Yimou had been able to make those films because his international reputation brought in foreign financing—from Japan for *Ju Dou,* Hong Kong/Taiwan for *Raise the Red Lantern*—yet this capacity for independence only made worse his relations with Chinese film authorities.

Zhang Yimou's most recent film, *The Story of Qiu Ju* (1992), is thus also a story of the director's reconciliation with the powers that be in China. His first work (as he notes below) set in contemporary China chronicles the struggles of a peasant woman (portrayed by Gong Li) to gain redress from China's bureaucracy and justice system after a village official has injured her husband in the groin. Though it retains the sumptuous color cinematography of his earlier films, Zhang Yimou's style here decisively shifts from symbolic to naturalistic, indeed, even quasidocumentary. Many of the performers are nonprofessionals, and some of the filming was done with hid-

---

From *Cineaste*, vol. 20, no. 1 (1993). Reprinted by permission.

den cameras. Politically, though hardly socialist realism, the film draws basically a favorable picture of patient Chinese officials striving for ethical and
humane solutions in a peasant society where people are capable of stubborn
pride but also quiet heroism. After he made *The Story of Qiu Ju*, Zhang Yimou's two previously banned films were released in China and warmly received by critics and audiences. *Cineaste* interviewed Zhang Yimou about the
new film (as well as some lesser known aspects of his earlier work) on the
occasion of its screening at the New York Film Festival; Vivian Huang provided the translation.

C I N E A S T E :   *To begin, let's go back to right after* Red Sorghum. *Your next film,*
Codename Cougar *(1989), is hardly known outside China. How did that work
come about?*

Z H A N G   Y I M O U :   At that time the whole Chinese film industry was
changing. The government was allowing private film enterprise. A friend of
mine wanted to make some money and found a subject he thought would
be profitable. The film didn't make any money, but it broke even in the end.
The subject matter was very sensitive. It's a fictional story about an airplane
hijacking between Taiwan and mainland China—a Taiwanese plane is forced
to land in mainland China, and the Taiwanese and Chinese governments
have to meet and do something about the situation. In the beginning, it
seemed like an interesting idea with a real point, but a lot of things couldn't
be shot, and the whole thing was censored. In the end, it became just a
purely commercial gun chase film and not that good.

C I N E A S T E :   *You personally played a role in bringing Chinese and Taiwanese
film cultures closer together with the well-known Taiwanese director Hou Hsiao-
Hsien serving as an executive producer on* Raise the Red Lantern. *What was the
background to that collaboration?*

Y I M O U :   Chen Kaige and I met Hou Hsiao-Hsien and [Taiwanese director]
Edward Yang in Hong Kong in 1985. We saw Hou Hsiao-Hsien's *The Time to
Live and the Time to Die* [1985] and Edward Yang's *Taipei Story* [1985]. They saw
Yellow Earth [1984, directed by Chen Kaige with cinematography by Zhang
Yimou]. We liked each other and became friends. Since then we have seen
each other often on different occasions. In 1988 during the Cannes Film Festi-
val, where [Chen Kaige's] *King of the Children* was in competition, we met

Hou Hsiao-Hsien and his producer Chiu Fu-Sheng. We started talking and joking about how we should work on a film together.

In 1990, after finishing *Ju Dou* I met Chiu Fu-Sheng again in Cannes and discussed the possibility of collaboration. I was about to start my next film, *Raise the Red Lantern*. I told him about the subject matter, and he was interested in it. He had the idea of having Hou Hsiao-Hsien's name on the film for commercial reasons, and he was only on the set a few times. He told me I should shoot the movie as I wanted to.

CINEASTE: *What was the attitude of the Chinese government to Taiwanese participation on* Raise the Red Lantern?
YIMOU: From a legal standpoint the co-production is not with Taiwan, it's with Hong Kong. The producer is from Taiwan but he set up a company in Hong Kong. The Chinese government welcomes Taiwanese investment. It was because of Taiwanese law that, in order to get a mainland Chinese film shown in Taiwan, it had to appear as if coming form a third party, from Hong Kong or Japan.

CINEASTE: *Some American reviewers have seen* The Story of Qiu Ju *as a completely new departure for you, others as consistent with your previous work. Which is it to you?*
YIMOU: In terms of film language or film style, it's totally different from my previous work. Of course, there are inner connections among all my films; the mentality remains consistent. But if you looked at *The Story of Qiu Ju* by its "look," you might not recognize it as my work. Looking at it on the screen, there are a lot of changes.

CINEASTE: *What specifically?*
YIMOU: My previous films are more deliberately designed, more abstract, more symbolic. The dramatic tension is much stronger. The subject matter is set in earlier times, further away from today's issues. The connection between their stories and contemporary life is rather distant. *The Story of Qiu Ju* is vice versa on everything. Where the others were distant, this one is very close to contemporary life. I purposely did this. When I designed this film, I was thinking about what I did before and wanted to do things in a reverse way. Just like the two sides of your hand, it's completely different.

Raise the Red Lantern is the best example to compare to *The Story of Qiu Ju*:

it is the most symbolic, the most designed, the most distant in time, of all my previous films. Yes, there are consistencies, for example in the use of the color red but even that's different. The red in this film is not for symbolic or abstract purposes. It's part of life, the peasant's life. It's an aspect of reality.

CINEASTE: *Critics have compared the style of* The Story of Qiu Ju *to Italian neo-realism or to Chinese cinema of earlier generations. Did you have any such associations in mind when making the film?*

YIMOU: My crew and I didn't think about neo-realism or old Chinese movies. We thought about the problem of contemporary Chinese film, about the two major problems of Chinese films today. First of all, they're too fake. No matter what kind of political purpose they have had, they have been made to look really fake. When people in a movie eat, it doesn't look like they're eating. When they sleep, they're not sleeping. When they speak, they're not speaking. The second problem is pretentiousness, alienation from reality. I hope this film will provide an accurate concept of what a film could be.

CINEASTE: *Do you have examples of individual films or filmmakers?*

YIMOU: No, when we were making the film we were talking about the fakery, the pretentiousness of Chinese film today as a body. I had a strong feeling about current Chinese film, especially in the last year or two. Chinese film is going backward. It's not like the time when we were making *Red Sorghum* and *The Old Well* [1986, directed by Wu Tianming with Zhang Yimou as the co-cinematographer and leading performer]. The whole industry then was more active and trying to do something. Now they are just going backward. In the last couple of years there have been too many cheap quality films. It messes up everything. The standard keeps going down. We hope we can have a certain influence on Chinese film, to let people know what the ideal of film is, which direction it should be going.

CINEASTE: *How did Chinese audiences and critics respond to what you were trying to do?*

YIMOU: They liked the film very much. It got good reviews with a lot of articles talking about it. It made people think about Chinese film. They used this film to compare with other Chinese films, even the previous work of the Fifth Generation filmmakers.[1] Because of this film a lot of people started to discuss how they should make a movie—though not that they should all follow the style of the film.

CINEASTE: *Is there a difference between the way Western critics read your work and how the Chinese people and critics regard it?*

YIMOU: According to what I heard in Venice [where *The Story of Qiu Ju* won the top prize at the 1992 Venice Film Festival] and also here, I think that the Western reviewer basically understands me. This film is simple and straight-forward. People generally look at the film as a story of human relationships. I think it is very universal. The difference between Western and Chinese crit-ics is that, when Chinese critics talk about this movie, they also compare it with contemporary Chinese movies. The Western film reviewers cannot talk about this because they don't see many Chinese films.

CINEASTE: *Do Chinese reviewers talk about this film in relation to contempo-rary Chinese problems?*

YIMOU: The Chinese film reviewer cannot write on everything.

Endnote

1. Chinese film history is recounted as a story of filmmaking generations. The term "Fifth Generation" describes the new filmmakers of the 1980s, many of whom entered Beijing Film Academy together when it reopened in 1978 after the Cultural Revolution. These include Zhang Yimou and Chen Kaige and such others as Tian Zhuangzhuang, direc-tor of *Horse Thief* (1986).

Of Gender, State, Censorship, and Overseas Capital: An Interview with Chinese Director Zhang Yimou

MAYFAIR MEI-HUI YANG/1993

ZHANG YIMOU STUDIED AT the Shaanxi Academy of Arts in Xi'an and graduated in 1982 from the Central Film Academy in Beijing. He is the most internationally acclaimed of the "Fifth Generation" of young filmmakers in China, the first group of students to graduate from the Beijing Film Academy after a long interruption during the Cultural Revolution (Berry 1991:116; Rayns 1991; Mason 1989). "Fifth Generation" films include those such as director Chen Kaige's *Yellow Earth (Huang tudi)*, a story about miscommunication between a communist soldier and a peasant girl (Yau 1991), and *King of the Children (Haizi wang)*, set in Yunnan province about a teacher trying to reach peasant school children (Chow 1992). Huan Jianxin weaves a Kafkaesque tale of bureaucratic intransigence and paranoia in *The Black Cannon Incident (Heipao shijian)* and *Horse Thief (Daomazei)* by Tian Zhuangzhuang verges on an ethnographic film of Tibet. Peng Xiaolian's *Women's Story (Nuren de gushi)*, about three peasant women who escape unhappiness in the village and travel together to the city, is one of the few Chinese films to express sisterhood among women (Berry 1989; Kaplan 1989).

In 1988, while at Xi'an Film Studio, Zhang Yimou's made his first feature film, *Red Sorghum (Hong gaolang)* (Wang 1991, Yang 1990), which won him a prize at the Berlin Film Festival. Two other films, *Ju Dou,* released in 1990, and *Raise the Red Lantern (Da hong denglong gaogao gua)*, released in 1991 (Zhang 1992; Tang

---

From *Public Culture*, 5:2 (Summer 1993), pp. 297–313. Copyright 1993. All rights reserved. Reprinted by permission of Duke University Press.

1992), were nominated for Best Foreign Language Film at two consecutive Oscar ceremonies. *The Story of Qiu Ju* won the grand prize at the Venice Film Festival in 1992, and Gong Li won the best actress award (World 1992).

Many of the Fifth Generation films of the 1980s were set in the desolately dry areas of Shaanxi, Gansu, Qinghai, and other poor provinces of the Northwest, thus acquiring the classification "Western films" (*Xibu pian*). This category describes films set in the remote western regions of China, away from the population centers of the eastern seaboard, where the simplicity and rawness of life provide a fertile ground for cultural critique and exploring questions of existence, meaning, and history, questions not sanctioned by a state intent on using film as an instrument for moral-political education.

Most Chinese film-goers have not been enamored of Fifth Generation experimental films, preferring to watch films with stronger storylines and melodramatic expressions, such as family dramas from Taiwan, the films of the popular Shanghai director Xie Jin, and kung-fu action films from Hong Kong. Zhang Yimou's *Red Sorghum* was the only Fifth Generation film to rank among the highest in number of film copies (*kaobei*) sold throughout the country. In 1988–89, box office admissions numbered 75,682,000 in China that year (Lai 1990). This was probably because the film won the 1988 Berlin Film Festival Prize, the most prestigious international award any Chinese film had at that time received, and this honor piqued popular curiosity about the film.

The period 1989–91, after the Tiananmen tragedy, saw a political tightening of the realm of "ideology" (*yishi xingtai*). During this time, the state financed several big-budget films on the history of the Chinese Communist Party to mark its seventieth anniversary as well as films on other moral-political educational themes. Cinema attendance, which had been on a steady decline (Berry 1991, 115) after the entry of television into most urban homes in the 1980s, continued to fall. To ensure good attendance at screenings of political films, the state issued "free" cinema tickets to urban residents through local work units, which were often aid for by the work units themselves.

It was also during this period that Zhang's next two films, *Ju Dou* and *Red Lantern*, were forbidden to be shown in China, although (on the basis of what I heard in Xi'an and Shanghai in early 1992) some city people managed to see *Ju Dou* on videotapes smuggled into the country from Hong Kong. In July 1992, in a dramatic reversal, the government declared that Zhang's two films could henceforth be shown in China (Gu 1992b). This decision was no doubt made in order to complement Deng Xiaoping's recent tour of south China, where he made public exhortations to speed up the pace of reform and liberalization (Lin 1992:12).

It is reported that the state Bureau of Film (*Dianyingju*) in Beijing was willing to release these films but could not get authorization from its superior administrative office, the Ministry of Radio, Film, and Television (*Guangbo dianying dianshi Bu*) (Xiao 1992:15). It was only after Li Ruihuan, the popular carpenter-turned-high-level-official in charge of the powerful Propaganda Ministry of the Chinese Communist party (Wei 1992), personally viewed *Ju Dou* and said, "I think *Ju Dou* can definitely be screened publicly" that the Film Bureau dared to proceed (Xiao 1992:15). In his capacity as the highest official in charge of art, literature, and ideology, Li Ruihuan is also reported to have viewed *The Story of Qiu Ju* and praised it, ironically, as a film worth advocating through government "propaganda" (*xuanchuan*) channels (Xiao 1992).

Indeed there are now signs that China is poised on the threshold of a new era of cultural and artistic efflorescence, as well as the rapid development of a commercialized popular culture. At an Inner Mongolian arts festival in August 1992, Li Ruihuan publicly spoke out: "Literature and art serve the functions of entertainment, aesthetics, education, and other diverse purposes. It is not right [to expect] that every single literary and artistic product must serve the function of political education." In the Ministry of Culture Directive no. 36, sent down to lower-level governments the same year, Li also declared that henceforth state literary and cultural organizations are permitted to enter into joint ventures with foreign companies and to benefit from Hong Kong, Taiwan, and foreign capital investments, technology, and experience. He urged that occupations in cultural production must now be integrated into the market economy (Wei 1992:9).

In early March 1992, I traveled by bus with Chinese friends from the city of Xi'an to the provincial town of Bao Jin in Western Shaanxi Province. We were going to visit director Zhang Yimou, who was shooting his fifth film, *The Story of Qiu Ju (Qiu Ju daguansi)*, and Gong Li, the star actress of all his films. The interview reconstructed here is the result of three days and nights on interviewing Zhang and observing him at work in the hotel that served as his on-site residence and film production and editing center. It also includes some statements he made in late March 1992 at the press conference in Hollywood for directors of foreign films nominated for the Academy

Award for Best Foreign Language Film. I have clustered questions around a few central themes or topics rather than adhere to the natural and tangential sequence of conversation so as to highlight some key issues of art and politics in China today.

Interview

Y [YANG]: *I've noticed that in all your films you use women to make a statement. Why?*

Z [ZHANG YIMOU]: It was really coincidental. All my films come from novels. It just so happens that these novels say things through women. This also fits in with my own sensibilities. Somehow this is in the air. What I want to express is the Chinese people's oppression and confinement, which has been going on for thousands of years. Women express this more clearly on their bodies (*zai tamen shenshang*) because they bear a heavier burden than men.

[At a 1992 Academy Awards press conference in Hollywood, Zhang Yimou described *Red Lantern* in this way: "This is a story about a few women and their tragedy. It doesn't matter whether they are good or bad, they deserve sympathy (*tongqing*). I wish less tragedy would befall their lives."]

Y : *Do you think that in the past 30–40 years, with so many political campaigns turning people against each other, women now stand for the soft and warm qualities people long for in relationships? Do you think the incredible popularity recently of the Taiwanese film* Mama, Love Me Again (Mama zai aiwo yici) *is due to this longing?*

[This was a production that elicited audience indifference in Taiwan but in 1990 and 1991 stirred up a storm of emotions in the mainland audience when it played to packed theaters of sobbing women and men, young and old. It tells the story of a boy who is separated in a heart-rending way from his mother by a cruel mother-in-law. It was the fourth most well-attended film of 1990, after *Jiao Yulu, Zhou Enlai,* and *Mao Zedong and His Sons*, all political films whose attendance were helped by the state's distributing free tickets. Therefore, *Mama* can be seen as the film that actually enjoyed the most popular demand. A few workers in Xi'an told me that it was the first film in China for which cinema box offices sold tissue paper as well as tickets.]

z : I have not actually seen this Taiwan film, but I've heard it's popular. One can see it the way you describe, but I believe the Chinese people's oppression has been going on much longer—for thousands of years. The Revolution has not really changed things. It's still an autocratic system (*zhuanzhi*), a feudal patriarchal system (*fengjian jiazhangzhi*). A few people still want to control everything and instill a rigid order.

That's why I was so excited when I discovered the walled gentry mansion [where *Red Lantern* was filmed], which is hundreds of years old in Shanxi Province. It's high walls formed a rigid square grid pattern that perfectly expresses the age-old obsession with strict order. The Chinese people have for a long time confined themselves within a restricted, walled space. Democracy is still very far off, and it will be slow in forming here. We have a historical legacy of extinguishing human desire (*miejue renyu*).

y : *This certainly comes out in* Ju Dou. *They can't make public their love. I have an interpretation of the film that I'd like to try out on you. Do you think the film can be interpreted this way: The old man represents oppressive tradition? Ju Dou and Tianqing dare to go against tradition and create a small happy world of their own. They make revolutions, so to speak. As a man, Tianqing is more reluctant to break the old rules because he is more invested in them. But Ju Dou, as a woman, has nothing to lose with the old system, so she's more bold. When Tianbi is born, they have high hopes for the future, a new era is dawning. But they cannot escape the oppressive tradition, especially when they give birth to a bit of a monster, who is just as concerned with punishing nonconformity as the old man. There's a point of recognition when Tianbi calls the old man "father"; each sees some of the other in himself. Do you think this reading works?*

z : Sure, that's one way to look at it. Tianbi the boy is weird because he is the product of an abnormal relationship, which is very twisted and distorted (*niuqu*). As he grows up, all around him is secrecy, so he does not speak. Tianbi calls the old man "father" because he has to. In those days, his real parents would be put to death if it were found out. Even down to the 1920s it was that strict. So you see how horrible this system is.

y : *Back to the setting for* Red Lantern. *What kind of place is this mansion?*

z : The compound belonged to a wealthy merchant and his four sons. They all lived there with their wives and families. [Each son had one wife.] He was very strict about drinking, gambling, and licentiousness. In the Republican period [1911–49], they had 160 servants and sixteen water carriers working twenty-four hour days. He was good to the local people. Whenever anyone had a special family occasion for celebrating, they would get to send one able-bodied person to his mansion and carry away as much grain as he could. That's why the local people supported the family and protected the mansion during the Cultural Revolution.

Y : *Yet it seems to me that* Red Lantern *is much more directly political than the others. The politics is much more clear and systematically argued.*
z : Yes, I agree.

Y : *Were the lanterns originally in Su Tong's novel (Su 1990; Li 1992)?*
z : No, the lanterns were my idea, to give a concrete form to their oppression.

Y : *You make your tragedies very beautiful.*
z : [*nodding*] When tragedy is "made aesthetic" (*meihua*), then it is all the more overpowering.

Y : *In all your films, the women possess a spirit of resistance* (fankang jingshen*).*
z : Yes, they do. In *Qiu Ju*, it's about a woman who comes to recognize her own self-worth (*ziwo jiazhi*), a woman who realizes that she controls her own fate.

[*Qiu Ju* is Zhang's first major film set in present-day China, about a peasant woman who goes from office to office up the bureaucratic ladder, seeking official redress and apology for a village cadre's mistreatment of her and her husband. The film is adapted from a recent short story by Chen Yuanbin entitled "Ten Thousand Litigations" (1991). At the actors' meeting held the day before the interview, the following interchange between Gong Li and Zhang Yimou took place:]

G [GONG LI]: [*cross and impatient with Zhang Yimou*] My role is to play Qiu Ju, but I myself still can't understand why Qiu Ju keeps on pursuing this matter, even though she's received formal monetary reparations from the cadre. You need to make the reason clearer to the audience, otherwise they will think this woman is being unreasonable, pestering people endlessly.

z : [*addressing Gong Li*] There is no danger in that; two scenes show the village cadre to be very nasty and imperious toward Qiu Ju. The audience will
side with Qiu Ju. It will be clear to them who is the weak party (*qianzhe*).
[*addressing Yang*] The matter that Qiu Ju is pursuing is very small but enough
to have the law interested in it, but Qiu Ju keeps on persistently confronting
officials, going from the village level to township level to county level to
prefecture level, all the way to the city of Bao Ji, almost to the highest level
of the whole province. She's been compensated, but she is still not at peace
with herself (*mei dedao xinglishang pingheng*) about it. What she's angry about
is the cadre's contemptuous attitude toward ordinary people. If the matter
were a big one, a life-and-death thing, then everyone would immediately
understand her. But since the matter is so small, the audience will be made
to try and figure out why Qiu Ju is doing this, so then they will have to
approach the matter from a new and different angle.

y : *From listening in on your actors' meeting yesterday, I gather that the audience
you have in mind is Chinese?*
z : Yes. I don't understand a Western audience's taste. It's a pity I've seen so
few first-run movies from abroad. Each year it's probably only ten at most.
It's difficult to get access to them. Since I started shooting *Qiu Ju*, I have not
seen one foreign film in six month's time. That's why I ask friends returning
from abroad to bring some in [on videotape], but they have to get through
customs. About the only opportunity I have of seeing foreign films is when I
go abroad to attend foreign film festivals to collect prizes and things. Then,
in between humoring people who insist on my participating at their social
engagements, I get some time for myself to watch films. I figure that the most
important thing is for me to get my films made.

y : *When you make a film, what kind of people do you think of as your audience?
Peasants? City people? Intellectuals?*
z : It's not like that; I have a general audience in mind. It's not as if, for this
film I think of peasant, and for another film I think of intellectuals. But I
may think of certain scenes or parts of a film as appealing especially to a
group. I understand peasant pretty well; I was one for three years during the
Cultural Revolution.

[Indeed, Zhang played a very convincing peasant, Sun Wangquan, the leading role in Wu Tianming's 1987 film *Old Well (Lao Jing)*, which won the grand prize and best male actor award at the Tokyo Film Festival (Wang 1988).]

Y : *When I watched you editing, it seemed you were always thinking about the audience.*
Z : Yes, I do. One must always address an audience, but one must also not capitulate to them or totally give them what they want. You must preserve your individuality (*gexing*). It's best to go along with them, so as to get them to accept what you have to say.

Y : *When I saw Xie Jin's* Flowers Beneath the High Mountains (Gaoshanxia de huahuan) *[a 1984 film about heroic Chinese soldiers in the Sino-Vietnamese war], I was angry because I knew Xie Jin was manipulating my tears to promote patriotism. I felt totally controlled.*
Z : Yes, one shouldn't do that. I like Truffaut's *400 Blows*, also Godard's early films. Godard really has individuality; he does not compromise. I can appreciate that about him. He does not care about the audience. At a press conference in Cannes, I saw him and the reporters exchange insults. He told them they didn't understand his films because their cultural level was too low. But the last couple of Godard films I couldn't understand either.

Y : *Some people abroad say that you only cater to a Western audience. Is this true?*
Z : That's what the government here says too. It's really not fair, when they won't let my films be shown in China. So, they won't even let the Chinese people see if they like them or not. Instead, I'm only allowed to spread these "poisonous fumes" (*sanfa duqi*) abroad to foreigners—to weaken and harm them, I guess.

[The Chinese government considers his films to be unhealthy, fit only to be distributed abroad. In July 1992, after this interview, the government reversed its position and gave permission for *Ju Dou, Red Lantern,* and *Qiu Ju* to be shown in China.]

Y : *How strange and ironic, how tragic and funny, that your films are shown all over the world but Chinese people themselves cannot see it in their own homeland, not in the mainland or in Taiwan. Only in Hong Kong. Could you tell me how the film censorship system works?*

z : Take *Qiu Ju* for example; the Central Broadcasting, Film, and Television Ministry had to look over and approve the script before we even started shooting. They also looked at the finished product after editing and cutting, even though the film was financed abroad. If they don't like it, it can only be distributed abroad, but not domestically.

Once the Ministry approved this script, they sent a "document" (*wenjian*) [or official directive to lower administrative levels] from Beijing to Shaanxi provincial government, who then sent a document to Bao Ju City, who sent one to the county, and to the village. We rushed to this area to start shooting before they changed their minds.

In China today, novels surpass the level of films tremendously. This is because each year thousands of new novels and short stories are published, and no one can keep up with them, especially the government censors. Not even their own subordinates in their offices can keep up, so they just give up trying. That's why good novels get through the system, and that's why Chinese writers look down on filmmakers. I like to read novels and use them for my films. It's not the same with film. Only about 150 films are produced in the country each year. The film censors like to watch films for entertainment in their spare time. So they are able to restrict films much more.

I've never met any of my censors; I don't even know what they look like. It's back-to-back double-blind censoring (*bei kao bei shencha*) [where neither the censor nor filmmaker knows each other]. The process feels like a judge and others will not allow the defendant to participate in the deliberation proceedings. All the defendant gets is a formal piece of paper, either a few sentences or several pages saying why the film was accepted [*playfully mimicking bureaucratic language*]: "This film accurately expresses the healthy relationship between cadres and the masses in socialism," and so forth. Or it will state why the film was rejected, what the offensive scenes were, and so on. Those who get through are elated because now their work can be shown. Those whose films receive a death sentence are crestfallen, especially their film studios because they have invested so much money in the film. Chinese films are not like Western films. They are neither a commodity nor a work of art—they belong in the realm of "ideology." That's why they are guarded so heavily—they know that film is a powerful medium for influencing thought.

Y :   *How have your films been financed?*
z :   *Red Sorghum* was produced by Xi'an Film Studio. *Ju Dou* relied on Japanese money. *Red Lantern* and *Qiu Ju* are both financed by the Taiwanese businessman Chiu Fu-Sheng.

[Chiu Fu-Sheng is known in the international Chinese community as a visionary "art film producer" (*yishu dianying zhipianren*) (Gu 1992a). He made his fortune, among other things, as the sole distributor of Columbia Pictures videotapes in Taiwan. His multinational film corporation ERA, based in Hong Kong, has financed two Chinese films that won the Venice Film Festival prize: *City of Sadness* (1989) by Taiwanese director Hou Hsiao-Hsien and Zhang's *Qiu Ju.*

In late March 1992, at a dinner for Zhang Yimou in Monterey Park, California. Chiu spoke to Ah Cheng, a writer from the Mainland, and me and waxed eloquent to the future of Chinese film: "The twenty-first century will be the Asian century. The world saw the power of Portugal and Spain in the sixteenth and seventeenth centuries, then France in the eighteenth, then England in the nineteenth, and the U.S. in the twentieth. Next it will be Asia's turn. The Asian pacific counties have the world's highest economic growth rates: Thailand, Indonesia, Malaysia, Korea, Taiwan, Singapore, Hong Kong, all of them. And there are Chinese living in all of these countries. So Chinese films will be a major cultural force in these places." Indeed, at the 1992 Academy Awards press conference in Hollywood, Zhang Yimou pointed out the Chinese film world's increasing turn overseas. "Now more and more Mainland Chinese realize that China is really three areas: the Mainland, Taiwan, and Hong Kong. Amongst directors, there is a great deal of contact and exchanges across these three areas."]

z :   The contract we signed [Chiu, Zhang, and the Ministry of Film] had it written in that the film producers, Chiu's company, have the right of ownership and the right to distribute the films abroad. But the contract also said that the films must pass through both preproduction and postproduction censoring, and the government will decide whether or not they can be shown domestically. With *Ju Dou*, the censors just put it aside and sat on it. No decision has been made [in two years' time], which amounts to a "no."

Y :   *Do you think overseas money has helped or hindered your work?*
z :   Yes, it has helped. The pressure from abroad on the government has made a difference on their behavior. And I couldn't have shot my last few films without outside money.

Y : *What do you think is the most important problem with Chinese films today?*
Z : They are so fake (*xujia*), they are overdramatic, and the actors do not act like they are people living life but like they are playing out a story. The acting is forced and staged. Chinese films do not show a deep examination or understanding of the reality Chinese people live in. In the past three years, there's been a regression (*daotui*) in Chinese films. None of them have attained, let alone surpassed, the level of realism of *In the Wild Mountains* (*Ye Shan*) or *Old Well* (*Lao Jing*). [The first film was made by Yan Xueshu in 1985, the second by Wu Tianming in 1987. Both films were Xi'an Film Studio productions about the lives of poor peasants in contemporary northwest China.]

In *Qiu Ju*, I'm really going in a new direction. I want to make a statement. This film is really very different from my other ones; it's like nothing I've ever done before. It's like a documentary film. I'm aiming for a natural and real look, no dramatic stuff. It's going to be more extreme in its realism than either *In the Wild Mountains* or *Old Well*. They were pretty realistic, but they still had lots of staged drama cut into natural shots. *Qiu Ju* is mostly natural. Most of it is natural scenes, which are wrapped around a few staged scenes. Fifty percent of the film was shot secretly; people didn't see the camera. The characters are played by real people: peasants, policemen, judge, and so on. We only used four professional actors. The cameras were hidden from view, and tiny microphones were attached to people's clothing. Like the marketplace scene we just shot. We got there at 5:00 a.m. and climbed onto the roof to hide the mike. We're editing with a 35-to-1 proportion [of film shot to film used]. Most Chinese films are 4 to 1 because studios can't afford to use up that much film. Xi'an Film Studio as a rule that you must do a 3.5 to 1. We can get away with 35 to 1 because we're shooting 16mm, not 35mm. This way the price comes out about the same. Later we'll take the film to Japan and transfer it to 35mm. It won't affect the quality.

Y : *Why do you use so few professional actors?*
Z : Professional actors are not appropriate for this film. When they are next to real people, it shows. They are trained to be theatrical, but this film does not want them to break out crying, to act heartbroken, or to jump up and down with glee. So this film has been a great challenge for Gong Li. Also, the film is done in Shaanxi dialect. This is because we have so many peasants in it that when the professional actors speak [in] Mandarin, it really clashes with them, so we thought we might as well make everyone speak [in]

Shaanxi dialect. We'll put subtitles in for those who don't understand Shaanxi dialect.

[Zhang's directions to three members of his cast, given during an actors' meeting the previous day, gives a flavor of how he tries to achieve the quality of realism in Qiu Ju. Besides Gong Li, one actor was a local man who worked in a local theatre troupe in Bao Ji. He had a wrinkled face with a wispy white beard, making him very convincing as the innkeeper where Qiu Ju was staying. The other man was in real life a lawyer in Bao Ji.

"Make your acting a part of life. The kind of acting I want does not take the setting as mere backdrop for the actors. What I want is for you to dissolve yourselves into the setting, to become a part of it. Don't treat your acting as a task (*renwu*) given to you. In too many films the vice-director gives a task to an actor to walk by in the background, and it never looks real; it just likes like the person has a task to accomplish."

"When you are sitting in the eating stall at the market and when you get the order to start, don't immediately look at each other to say your lines. Act as if you were there to have a meal, put some vinegar in your noodles, look around at people, examine the content of the wok the cook is leaning over. Someone might unexpectedly come over and ask you a question. You have to be ready to deal with anything unexpected. There will be three cameras hidden in different places. If you discover one, don't pay attention to it. The mike is hidden in the middle of the table, so make sure you aim in that direction when you speak. The vice-director will at first sit with you. He will have a radio in his ear; we will give the order to him when the cameras start shooting. He'll say to you 'start,' then get up and walk away. After he has left about six seconds, then you start on your own; no further notice will be given. Then the vice-director will come back, and we'll do this take at least five times. Don't eat any of the noodles between takes because you'll stuff yourselves to death. When we shot the peasants eating last time, they just kept on eating, so they had to each consume six large bowls of noodles. At first, they were very hungry, and you know how peasants can eat a lot, but after a while, they really felt bloated [*general laughter*]. Their roles were really well done— they acted just like regular people. They didn't even know where the cameras were."]

Y : *Do you think that Chinese film has to first master realism* (xieshi zhuyi, *[distinguished from the "socialist realism," shehui zhuyi xianshi zhuyi]) before it can go on to other styles of art, as in the West. In the nineteenth century, realism broke with an older, romanticized salon art, so that realism made possible such movements as impressionism, cubism, and abstract expressionism? So do you think you have to do realism to break with the official socialist realism?*

z :   Yes, it should be this way. For example, the peasants I worked with for this film—their main goal is to get enough to eat and creature comforts. How can you ask them to comprehend our talk [at a dinner the previous night] about people who gamble such huge amounts of money in Macao and lose hundreds of thousands of Hong Kong dollars? Many Chinese intellectuals and artists try to use Western so-called postmodernism (*hou xiandai zhuyi*) to address and encapsulate (*tao*) the Chinese situation. They take the Western-ers' urban maladies (*chensi bing*), the loneliness and pressures of life in advanced industrial society, and make Chinese characters express them. This is not a Chinese problem, we have not even gotten to that stage. So it's not appropriate to apply postmodernism to China. What we still need to do is oppose feudalism and liberate the self (*ziwo jiefang*).

Y :   *So you don't think postmodernism is relevant to China?*

z :   I think when Chinese do arrive at the level that the West is now in, China will probably not express the problem in the same way, or the problem will be encountered in a different way with a different set of problems because Chinese historical development has its own particular features.

Y :   *What do you mean by postmodernism?*

z :   Well, I really can't say for sure. I haven't read systematically about it. I've only read about it through translations and secondary sources.

Y :   *One feature of postmodernism, I think, is that it doesn't set up a clear opposition between tradition and modernity, to champion the latter.*

z :   What is its attitude toward tradition?

Y :   *It doesn't want to go back to tradition, but it doesn't reject it either, or would like to selectively integrate some of it.*

z :   A lot of young people today are like that. They are neither totally rejecting of tradition nor taken up with modernity. They just don't subscribe to any faith now.

Y :   *Yes, that's another feature of postmodernism—people no longer believe in grand explanations of history. What will your next film be?*

Z :   It will be about leather shadow puppetry in Shaanxi Province. [Xi'an Film Studio screenwriter] Lu Wei is working on the script. Chiu Fu-sheng is financing it again. It's the story of a peasant girl who falls in love with a young man who works on the village film team showing films to peasants. His father is an old puppeteer whose trade is losing an audience to film, and so he disapproves of their marriage. We haven't really decided on whether to set it in the present or the past.

Mayfair Mei-hui Yang teaches anthropology at the University of California–Santa Barbara. She has completed two-and-a-half years of fieldwork in China and has written on Chinese gift relations (*guanxi*) and their role in Chinese politics today.

Literature Cited

Berry, Chris. 1989. "China's New Women's Cinema." *Camera Obscura* 18, 4–41.

———. 1991. "Market Forces: China's 'Fifth Generation' Faces the Bottom Line." In *Perspectives on Chinese Cinema*. Chris Berry, ed. (London: British Film Institute), 114–25.

Chen, Yuanbin. 1991. "Wanjia susong" ["Ten Thousand Litagations"]. In *Xiao-shuo yuebao* [*Short Story Monthly*], no. 8.

Chow, Rey. 1992. "Male Narcissism and National Culture: Subjectivity in Chen Kaige's 'King of the Children.' " In *Camera Obscura* 25/26: 9–39.

Gu, Bilin. 1992a. "Huaren dianying xing daheng" ["The New Magnate of Chinese Films"]. *Zhongguo shibao* [*China Times Weekly*] 13 (29 March), 78–79.

———. 1992b. "Denglong gaogua, 'Fengzhen' nan fei" ["The 'Lantern' is Held High, the 'Kite' Has Trouble Flying"]. *Zhongguo shibao* [*China Times Weekly*] 34 (23 Aug.), 82–83.

Kaplan, Anne. 1989. "Problematizing Cross-Cultural Analysis: The Case of Women in Recent Chinese Cinema." *Wide Angle* 11 (no. 2), 40–50.

Lai, Quiyun. 1990. "What Do Chinese Film Audiences Appreciate?" *China Screen* 2.

Li, Rui. 1992. "Cong qiqie chengqun dao dahong denglong gaogaogua: zhuan fang xiaoshuo yuanzuozhe Su Tong" ["From 'Herding Wives and Concubines' to 'Raise the Red Lantern': An interview with the novelist Su Tong"]. *Zhongguo shibao* [*China Times Weekly*] 13 (29 March), 76–77.

Lin, Fan. 1992. "Weinyijie de chuntian heshi daolai?" ["When will the Spring for the Art and Literature World Arrive?"]. *Zhongguo shibao* [*China Times Weekly*] 35 (30 August), 12–13.

Mason, Marilynne S. 1989. "China's New Wave." *World Monitor*, March, 77–80.

Rayns, Tony. 1991. "Breakthroughs and Setbacks: The Origins of the New Chinese Cinema."

In *Perspectives in Chinese Cinema*, Chris Berry, ed. (London: British Film Institute), 104–13.

Su, Tong. 1990. "Qiqie chengqun" ["The Herding of Wives and Concubines"]. In *Shou Huo* [*Harvest*].

Tang, Ben. 1992. "Sejue, renjue he xinjue: ping dianying dahong denglong gaogaogua" ["Sexual Plunder, Human Plunder, and the Plundering of the Heart: A Review of 'Raise the Red Lantern' "]. *Shijie ribao* [*World Daily News*], 9 August.

Wang, Yeujin. 1988. "The Old Well: A Womb or Tomb? The Double Perspective in Wu Tianming's 'Old Well.' " *Framework* 35, 73–82.

———. 1991. "Red Sorghum: Mixing Memory and Desire." In *Perspectives in Chinese Cinema*, Chris Berry, ed. (London: British Film Institute), 80–103.

Wei, Ping. 1992. "Li Ruihuan gao da dongzuo zuofeng" ["Li Ruihuan Takes a Big Step to Sweep Out the 'Leftist Wind' "]. *Zhongguo shibao* [*China Times Weekly*] 35 (30 August), 9–11.

World Daily News [*Shijie ribao*]. 1992. "Qiu Ju da guansi lunde jingshijiang" ["'Qiu Ju Goes to Court, Wins the Golden Lion Award"]. 13 Sept.

Xiao, Wei. 1992. "Shisida dangqian, dalu wenyijie renshi fenqi fanzuo" ["Mainland Art and Literature World Turns Against the Left on the Eve of the Fourteenth Party Congress"]. *Zhongguo shibao* [*China Times Weekly*] 35 (30 August), 14–15.

Yau, Esther C. M. 1991. " 'Yellow Earth': Western Analysis and a Non-Western Text." In *Perspectives in Chinese Cinema*, Chris Berry, ed. (London: British Film Institute), 62–79.

Zhang, Jiaxuan. 1992. Dahong denglong gaogaogua: meiyou chuntian de beiju" ["Raise the Red Lantern: A Tragedy without a Spring"]. *Zhongguo shibao* [*China Times Weekly*] 13 (29 March), 74–75.

Zhang, Yingjin. 1990. "Ideology of the Body in 'Red Sorghum': National Allegory, National Roots, and the Third Cinema." *East-West Film Journal* 4 (June), 38–53.

Ten Years of Suppressed Energy: The Creative Path of Zhang Yimou

CHUN CHUN/1994

ZHANG YIMOU, BORN IN Xian in 1950, is a "Fifth Generation" Chinese director who displayed a strong interest in photography and design at an early age. In 1982, after graduating from the Beijing Film Academy, he joined the Guangxi Film Studio, and won cinematography awards for *Yellow Earth* and *The Big Parade* at the Chinese Golden Rooster Awards. He then expanded the scope of his Chinese film career. His debut directorship of *Red Sorghum* won the Golden Bear at the Berlin International Film Festival, after which his *The Story of Qiu Ju* won the Venice Film Festival's Golden Lion, all of which has caused him to rise the ranks of famous international directors.

At the beginning of the 1980s, a group of directors brought new light to the Chinese film world. They belong to the fifth generation of Chinese film directors, who experienced the hardship and turbulence of the Cultural Revolution and endured the burden of a ten-year dark period in film. Tempered by history, their works have been a clap of thunder, endlessly garnering world praise and repeatedly winning international honors. Zhang Yimou and Chen Kaige may be said to be the leaders of this group of Fifth Generation directors.

One point of difference between Zhang Yimou and Chen Kaige is that Zhang both directs and acts. We have the good fortune of being able to enjoy his performance as Meng Taifang in *A Terra Cotta Warrior* with Gong Li as

From *City Entertainment: Film Biweekly*, No. 394 (19 May 1994). Reprinted by permission. Translated by Stephanie Deboer.

the lead actress. Zhang Yimou is undoubtedly a good actor, but his talent really lies in directing. Not one of his works—from *Red Sorghum* to *Ju Dou*, *Raise the Red Lantern*, and *The Story of Qiu Ju*—have disappointed his audiences. He doesn't resemble Hou Hsiao-Hsien or Edward Yang's continuous heavy seriousness. The humorous new trails blazed by *The Story of Qiu Ju* in particular pleasantly surprised us. He has a resolute wildness, yet always understands how to utilize a fixed space to create an outstanding work that garners people's heartfelt admiration. He dares to challenge established and traditional moral values in a refined manner and, by no means, shouts himself hoarse. In his previous three works, he—mainly by means of adultery or sexual taboo, the most human and primeval of desires—has denounced unfounded moral dogma.

When I interviewed Zhang Yimou, I was actually at a loss—this is a director whom I've respected for a long time, yet had never interviewed. Each of his films coerces a feeling toward a country that's complicated and difficult to articulate, so I was deeply afraid of mistakenly touching on some sensitive point or harming some innocent bystander.

Many people have shown concern for the film, To Live. *How is its situation now?*
Judgement on *To Live* is only now being passed, and I don't know what the concrete situation is. I myself still haven't received any news.

In Hong Kong we've read a little information about it in the newspapers, which said that the authorities won't allow you to make a film for three years. Have they contacted you yet? What have they said about making films?
I still haven't personally received any message or statement.

Well, do you know whether or not Tian Zhuangzhuang or Zhang Yuan will ever be able to make films again?
I've also read this news in the newspaper—it was an official document of the Ministry of Broadcasting made public through the newspapers that said until their problems are resolved, they won't be allowed to make films. As for what kinds of problems need to be settled, I'm not sure because I don't understand the whole situation.

The films of China have been at a low ebb for a long time; the reasons are of course many, but have Chinese patterns of storytelling been a problem? When we watch

Hollywood films, they have an extremely clear international language—people of every location can understand and be pulled into it.
There have long been many reasons for this low ebb of Chinese film. It's not entirely for this reason because every country—every nationality—has its own unique way of telling stories. Of course, America's Hollywood is an exception because it's gone through many years of tempering to form a typical Hollywood style, to set up a mainstream model for world commercial film. As for mainland film, because it hasn't developed any fixed pattern, each director relies upon his or her own mode of thinking to tell a story—each person's style is different.

Have you had any problems with funding?
Of course we've had big problems. Because film isn't really prospering these days, every film studio must assume sole responsibility for its profits or losses; loss of capital only puts pressure on the labor force—commodity costs, every kind of expense, is getting higher, which causes the number of employees to drop. On the other hand, film audiences are also dropping. All kinds of sources of entertainment are continually on the rise, so people no longer focus on film when they look for entertainment. This has caused poor conditions for every film studio now—in many cases, they have no film to shoot, or they only shoot low budget films. Low budget films, on the whole, are inversely related to quality—high budget, high quality films just can't be made. China's film distribution system is now changing, but at present it's still in a difficult situation. Therefore, a significant problem is also that film studios don't receive money when they make films—a market of a billion people and they can't even regain their costs. Yet if you look at Hong Kong, its space is small and its population is only six million, but its film industry has still been self-sufficient for many years, and has even prospered—more so than France, Germany, England, or Japan. This is an outstanding example of success. You ask why a population of one billion still can't cover costs? There are so many reasons that I can't understand them all. In any case, distribution, audience, profit allocation, etc. are all reasons.

Are restrictions on themes a significant factor?
On the mainland, theme limitations are always present; they've already been around for ten years. They mainly consist of screenplay checks early on and the very last examination of the completed film. In this censor system, there

are of course many restricted zones into which we can't intrude—for example, anything anti-government or anti-party. This goes without saying; everyone knows they can't shoot these kinds of films. The overly violent is also included in these restricted zones.

Under such strict restrictions, what hope is there for dealing with themes when making movies on the mainland?
The areas about which we can shoot are still very flexible, so there's still a wide berth for themes. You can't say that because there's a censor system then there's no hope. If you look at these past years, despite restrictions having been this strict, quite a few good films have appeared. This goes to show that quite a few things can still be filmed.

Looking at your own films, each one-from Red Sorghum *to* Raise the Red Lantern-*has been more pessimistic than the previous. Why?*
I'm not so sure about that. *The Story of Qiu Ju* wasn't pessimistic, was it? [He laughs.] It's just that the themes are different. For example, I adapted *Ju Dou* and *Raise the Red Lantern* from fiction, and their original stories were trage-dies—only when they're made to make people sad can they be considered successful. If you leave the theater laughing, then I've failed completely.

What is the theme of To Live*?*
To Live is a story about one family over a number of decades. I feel that this family's story is representative of the experiences of ordinary Chinese peo-ple, so we made their story span from before liberation to the nineteen-sev-enties. From *The Story of Qiu Ju* and up to *To Live*, I've utilized contemporary settings and realistic cinematic techniques, although the methods of these two films aren't exactly the same. The distinguishing feature of *To Live* is that it pays attention to packaging and isn't like my earlier films with their com-paratively heavy material, composition, lighting, and posing. When I made *To Live*, these things weren't very important; I simply wanted to use a very popular method to tell a story, portray its characters, depict a family.

Is this a rather significant transformation for you? I'd say that The Story of Qiu Ju *is also extremely realistic.*
For *The Story of Qiu Ju*, I used a very stylistic method to emphasize its realism. Very few directors can use this method in making films—one could say it

utilizes an extreme method to film realistically, pushes realism to its most intense degree to achieve the most satisfactory level. This in itself is very different from my earlier painstakingly manipulative method of creating characters. I did this, of course, intentionally because I've always hoped to change often as a director because in simply transforming oneself frequently, one's point of view also becomes more varied. Moreover, *To Live* is also basically a tragedy, but into this tragedy we've added much more humor. it has many more humorous points than *The Story of Qiu Ju*.

You're the executive producer of The Great Conqueror's Concubine; *what have you contributed to this film—anything in particular?*
This film was directed by Stephen Shin, and my contribution was limited. I simply helped out as much as I could, only talking things over with them during meetings. I've just seen the preview, and based on this preview, I feel that this film was made very well, and it's very imposing. It has a large-scale, big-movie style. It isn't one of these recent popular Hong Kong martial arts films with people flying all over the place, gorgeous and illusory. Rather, it's a very realistic historical testimony with a very imposing, primeval, and boundless feeling. For a Hong Kong director not familiar with mainland life, he certainly confronts much difficulty; and considering this difficulty—it's not easy to achieve this degree—he grasps it well. Compared to *A Terra Cotta Warrior*, it might be more realistic, but it doesn't have the romanticism of *A Terra Cotta Warrior*; in its grand spectacle point-of-view and style, it's in no way inferior to *A Terra Cotta Warrior*. It portrays the great hero Xiang Yu rather desolately. It also depicts the story of four people—Xiang Yu, Liu Bang, Lu Zhi, and Yu Ji—and interprets their male/female emotional relationships from today's perspective; much of these relationships are built on power, personal interest, and wild ambition—they really have character. This perspective and starting point is very interesting. There isn't any tacit guarding of historical conventions. Of course, this shooting of a new angle on history is extremely difficult, so there are both successful and failed aspects. But to even think of this perspective is great.

Nowadays, are mainland television programs a big threat to film?
The majority of the mainland audience doesn't leave its door and simply watches TV at home. Only when a movie has a huge reception or causes a big controversy will audiences enter the movie theaters. Instead, those mi-

grant laborers watch movies the most, so some people say that they are what supports the entire mainland film industry. Because they don't have homes, they can only watch movies.

What do you think of Taiwanese film or of its directors such as Hou Hsiao-Hsien and Edward Yang?
They're all my good friends; I've always admired their films greatly. Anyone can see the success of their artistic explorations. Of course, they don't make mainstream, commercial films. I feel that my biggest impression when seeing their films is a feeling that Hong Kong, Taiwanese, and Chinese films—to a certain extent—are consistent in their expression and understandings of people's history. This demonstrates that we're all the same people. We're very similar in our perspectives and ways of looking at the world.

What points do you think are consistent?
It's different for each person. Take Hou Hsiao-Hsien, for example. His works are a kind of reflection that confronts the commercialism that surrounds them. This is extremely similar to us Fifth Generation directors. It's that we confront the revisions of history and confront revisions of society. The spirit of the people captured by these films are all similar in their hope to understand history from another point of view, to recognize Chinese people anew.

I really feel that Hou Hsiao-Hsien has an extremely deep affection for Chinese culture. Could it be that China, Hong Kong, and Taiwan are all alike with a large group of people who bear a heavy cultural burden?
I wouldn't say that it's a burden—a burden can become a negative thing. But there's definitely a large group of people like this who all have a great interest in Chinese traditional culture, history, and people. This is inevitable, and how they deal with it all depends upon each person's style.

As far as we know, we only see Chinese Fifth Generation directors receiving international awards or recognition. In your opinion, are there any successors to this group of people?
Right now, I still don't see any successors. Personally, I've always felt that this is strange. The Fifth Generation has already been around for over ten years—we graduated in 1982—but we still haven't seen a strong and powerful sixth generation. Maybe it's because this Fifth Generation group didn't make

any progress during the ten years of the Cultural Revolution—this culture was suppressed for ten years without any cultural development. So, when reform and opening came into bloom, we faced the world with strong self-sufficiency and naturally became a central force in society. This hasn't been true only for film. China's centralist forces of today have all emerged from the ten years of cultural suppression, and because of this ten-year suppression, their capabilities have been very strong. The situation today is that the next generation hasn't had this "opportunity" of history, and hasn't accumulated strong capabilities—this has been an inevitable biological process. On the other hand, young people of today are facing an opening up of the world; they can see many things, yet can't find their own direction. They aren't as strong as we are at determining the self, at establishing a strong identity and strength of expression. It's not that young people don't have artistic talent, but that in our excessively multifarious society, they simply get lost in the complexity of this dazzling and tempting world. So it's rather rare that they truly express a creation based on inner impulse; they rather consider the practical and material problems of life. Our creations are only spurred by a kind of feeling that has to be expelled.

I really agree with what you say. I remember when I came to the mainland in '83, every publishing house had so many outstanding works—the publication of original Chinese as well as translated works was all lively. A large group of writers came to the force then, but it seems that there's only Jia Pingwa in literary circles now.
I think that money worship was the inevitable result of reform and opening. This is a good thing from the point of view of the government because people can first be prosperous. From the point of view of culture, this of course doesn't work. But I think that this situation will pass; once people have achieved a certain level of monetary contentment, then there'll be people who won't attach so much importance to money, and culture will move forward again.

Interview with Zhang Yimou

HUBERT NIOGRET/1994

To Live *covers four decades in numerous places over very different time periods and a lot of secondary characters.*
This is indeed a more difficult movie than any film I have done before. I wanted to do something different from my previous movies and I find it more interesting.

When was the novel published? What did it represent?
The novel was published at the end of 1992. I read it at the beginning of 1993 and liked it. Yu Hua is very famous in China; he is an avant-garde writer, but *To Live,* his first realist novel, was not very successful. It is less known than the novels of other writers which I adapted before, such as *Red Sorghum* (*Hong goaliang*). I loved the story because it talked about simple people, a very ordinary Chinese family, and their relationships: one could see the people's evolution through life, their attitudes, and not too much political and social background. History was secondary while the individual and the family were in the first plan. It is an aspect to which the directors of the Fifth Generation did not give much attention, and I wanted to break this pattern, to pay more attention to the individual and the family. I started to film it at the beginning of 1993.

How did Yu Hua and Lu Wei develop the script? You are not mentioned, but did you participate to its writing?

From *Positif* #410-02 (July–August 1994). Translated by Lenute Giukin.

I always participate in the writing of my movies, from the beginning to the end, even if my name does not appear. Yu Hua wrote a first version of the script. After he left, Lu Wei wrote the second version.

Did the novel cover more events in time or depth?
I reduced the time period from the novel because the story unfolds to the present day. I chose to stop in the seventies. But the novel starts, like my movie, in the forties.

The forties and fifties are pretty negative with positive episodes (the main character is ruined, but receives a box with shadow puppets; he is recruited by the national-ists, but liberated by communists), while the sixties and seventies are mostly posi-tive, with some negative aspects (the death of the child and mother in labor).
I did not think about it. This reversal negative/positive and after positive/negative is true, but it was not intended willingly. It is simply the evolution of the characters.

There is a big irony in the film: the main character's life is saved because he is ruined, and the character that took his house is condemned as reactionary. On the other hand, the two prominent characters of the Cultural Revolution period are a mute and a lame person.
There is a lot of humor in the movie, but I don't want to make any judgment. What matters is how the public feels about it.

At the end of your film, the characters become tragicomic and absurd, as in the hospital sequence: the guards are incompetent, the doctor is taken out of prison but cannot fulfill his duty. You obviously favor these aspects.
This was a deliberate choice on my part, especially as a reaction to other movies that were made about this historic period of China; they are very somber and heavy and emphasize the suffering of people or the problems of intellectuals. I wanted to show things from a different point of view with this addition of humor and the absurd, so the public would experience some-thing else.

In Qiu Ju, *(Qiu Ju da guansi), the absurd comes from the succession of different situations. In* To Live *the humor is felt in the movement of things, in the film's dynamic. Is this a direction you would like to explore?*

There are different forms of humor in the two films. I chose a more absurd humor in *To Live*, again as a reaction to the films about the Cultural Revolution which lacked humor; this style in *To Live*, I like a lot. But again, it depends on the script and the novel I adapt for the screen. In this case, the humor matched the subject well, but this is not always the case and it really depends on the encounter with the text.

The final sequence is based on hope, but it is also very critical: while animals become bigger in the first story, in this final sequence the bull does not grow any-more . . . it is dreadful. These people survive.
I did not try to be critical on purpose. It is true that the first time the father tells the story, after the bull comes the communism; people can "eat meat." The second time when the child asks the question, the grandfather does not know how to answer, and he has a moment of hesitation. By ending this way I did not intend to criticize contemporary society, I just told the story without any ulterior motive.

Wasn't it necessary to go through "serious" films in order to be able to talk now with humor about this period?
Of course, "serious" and more dramatic films allowed this one. It is always the same process: because with a foundation we can evolve to something else. Every movie is another stage compared to the preceding ones.

The novel of Yu Hua spreads out all the way to the present time. The films of the Chinese directors of the Fifth Generation are all preoccupied with history which is fantastic, but they stop at the death of Mao Zedung, and To Live, *a little bit earlier. Why? Can't they go further?*
It is possible to make movies on the period that follows Mao's death. I stopped in 1947 because the novel was not as good for the later period: everyone dies, all the secondary characters, only the main character, who becomes an old gentleman, is alive, and a cow. I thought that the public would accept this succession of deaths with difficulty, that it would be discouraged. It seemed to me heavy and excessive. Today in China, the films that present the period after Mao's death are not necessarily good films; not all are distributed, and even less selected by Westerners. You will probably not have the occasion to see them, but there are many. It is also true that I did not yet deal with this period.

None of these films talks about one of the reasons of the Cultural Revolution, the
opposition between Mao Zedung and Deng Xiaoping, the so-called symbol of the
capitalist reactionary, who reappeared later.
I don't see things this way. I don't think this relates so closely to the political
history. If the movies representing those years are less numerous, it is because
people like me are less interested by this period. There is a more dramatic
aspect, more interesting when characters go through complex periods in
which transformations are sudden-for example when the character is recruited by the Guomindang after he finds himself in the communist liberation army. In what concerns this historical period and from the authorial
point of view, one could describe human destiny very dramatically with frequent and rapid upheavals. Cinematically, this produces interesting things.
In the last twenty years, the events were not so dramatic, the times being
more peaceful. Maybe it is less dramatic to portray human lives.

The shadow theatre is a great idea, a truly cinematic idea that is not in the novel.
Neither was the dyeing from Ju Dou *in the novel. One could hardly imagine* Ju
Dou *without the dyeing, and without the shadow theater* To Live *would seem*
impossible. How did the idea appear and how was it integrated?
When making movies, I always want to add visual elements to the story that
would bring something new and make it flow better. The colored fabrics
from *Ju Dou* and the Chinese shadows in *To Live* have this function. One
cannot just tell a story, a film also needs appealing, interesting elements, but
always in the service of the story. In *To Live* when the main character tells
the story to his grandson for the second time, I intended to make him sing
again an opera song in the end; but I told myself that I should not exaggerate
or insist too much, that I should on the contrary, pay attention to the balanc-
ing of these elements. And when I look back at the way I used the dyeing in
Ju Dou, I think I exaggerated it a little at that time. Nowadays, I know how
to be more moderate, but these are elements that make movies beautiful
to see.

It is the production . . .
Yes.

The shadow theatre is a traditional and popular form of art. Did you have any
special relation with the shadow theatre, especially in your childhood?

As a child I went to see such shows and even bought some cheap puppets to play simple shadows. In China, it is not a very widespread popular art, except for certain regions like Shanxi. There, it is a very ancient art, but unfortunately, an art which tends to disappear rapidly because the artists who knew it well are now very old. They have difficulties in training disciples, the young not being interested in this form of art. They prefer to dance in discos. Thinking at its imminent disappearance, we took advantage when shooting certain scenes from *To Live* and made a documentary about the shadow theatre in China.

In the last two years, many Chinese or Taiwanese films have the theatre as subject: Farewell My Concubine, The Puppet Master, Zhao le, Gambling for Pleasure. *Is this a fundamental aspect in the Chinese culture or a renewed interest in these forms of show from the people in their forties?*
I think it is really a coincidence and not a premeditated thing. But all the evoked arts have the common quality of being ancient and belong specifically to Chinese culture. Those who liked to see these shows still like them—the intellectuals or older people accustomed since their childhood with these types of shows—but there is no new public. Young people ignore them completely.

A certain number of dramatic events take place off screen in the film, on the soundtrack. For example: the sound of the liberation army soldiers' arrival—which one cannot see—when they are in the middle of the nationalist army cadavers; it is great.
Sometimes this is my choice, but other times this corresponds to the time period, to the reconstitution of the fifties. Up to the sixties, people were surrounded by sounds that came from speakers installed in the streets and constantly diffusing the propaganda, the political discussions. These sounds, which are not necessarily linked to the image, are always present even in the cemetery. Chinese people will always be sensitive to it because they experienced it; this was absent from my childhood, the speakers, the propaganda, the revolutionary songs. . . . In the movie, they stress even more the absurd aspect and bring me closer to the public.

You have a different cinematographer for this film, Lu Yue. For each of your films, you have a new remarkable one. You were a cameraman yourself; what freedom do

you give them on the set? The photography in this film is more complex than in the previous films due to the variety of places and time periods.
All the cameramen are my former classmates and I find them very good. There are others I have not worked with yet, so you will encounter more names in my future movies. I like to work with them because we know well each other. Lu Yue was my best classmate when I was in the cinematography section at the Film Academy. Our collaboration starts with long discussions to clarify a maximum of aspects, exchange ideas, develop our strategy. During the shooting, I give them complete freedom to work as they like. I take care only of the actors' directing, and sometimes, if I feel that the image has to be modified to facilitate their work, I get involved, but only in that situation: the image has to be at the service of the actors' work. For every new film it is important for me to have a new approach to the image. Lu Yue, who filmed *To Live,* has a particular connection with France where he lived for five years. He decided later to return to China. His work attitude was reinforced by this "French experience": he is extremely conscientious and dedicated. It is a very appreciated thing in China nowadays and the whole team loves working with him. We will certainly work together again in the future.

The image of *To Live* is indeed complex compared to my previous films, but it connects better with the general public. My movies used to have a more esthetic "wrapping," closer to painting in some ways. This time, the difficulty was to make something simple but also adapted to the numerous changes in place.

Red Sorghum, Ju Dou, and Raise the Red Lantern *represent a first period partially formalist while* Qiu Ju, *and* To Live *constitute a second period, more realistic. In the last movies, the choices are more integrated.*
I agree with this division of my films. The first ones were more attached to form, colors and image, ignoring a little too much the actors and the characters' description. They favored estheticism. The last two films are centered more on the characters, on the individual story. It is the quality of my last two films that is missing in the first ones. In the future, I hope to reconcile these two aspects better, to save the form from the first movies while doing more precise and intense work on the characters. This would be a growth for me if I manage it.

Zhang Still at the Heart of Chinese Filmmaking

RONE TEMPEST/1995

RECENTLY, THE MARQUEE OF the Shanghai paradise theater here featured a large, painted panel advertising the showing of *To Live*—the critically acclaimed film directed by Zhang Yimou and starring Gong Li. Zhang, the intense genius, was portrayed broodingly in the foreground. The beautiful Gong Li, dressed in a traditional silk gown with high-button collar, demurred elegantly in the background.

Over the past decade, Zhang and Gong had built one of the world's most successful creative relationships. In film, he was Ingmar Bergman to her Liv Ullmann. Off-screen, although not married, she was Woodward to his Newman. They were mainland China's most fashionable couple. But there were two things wrong with this picture. First, after living together for years, Zhang and Gong recently broke up during the making of their newest collaboration in Shanghai. The split caused a sensation in the movie-crazy Hong Kong press and, according to reports, threatens to disrupt their longtime working relationship. Second, the movie *To Live* is supposed to be banned in China by the state propaganda department. So what was it doing on the marquee of the movie theater in one of Shanghai's elite neighborhoods, one full of high-ranking Communist officials?

When asked why they had a *To Live* poster on their marquee, the managers of the Paradise mumbles something about the film "coming soon," although there has been no hint of the government lifting its ban.

Told about the poster for *To Live*—which won a best actor award for star

From *Los Angeles Times* (27 February 1995). Reprinted by permission.

Ge You at the Cannes film festival—during an interview here, Zhang managed a smile. Though officially banned, the film is widely available on video, and some theatres somehow still manage to show it. "I went back to Xian," Zhang said, referring to the city in Shaanxi Province where he began his filmmaking career. "Everyone had seen it." This pleasant thought elicited a satisfied chuckle.

That's the way things are these days in China. Lots of rules. Inconsistent application. Just because something is banned (and China refused to nominate the film for best foreign language film for the Academy Awards) doesn't mean it is out of circulation. The U.S. government learned a lot about this condition in negotiations that led to Sunday's agreement with China on copyright, trademark, and patent infringements. Pirated American CDs and videos are everywhere. The laws banning them have been on the books, but . . .

Interviewed in his room at the no-frills hotel where his film crew is based in Shanghai for his latest film, Zhang Yimou appears small, almost frail. Patiently—the strain of all-night filming sessions showing in eyes that appear bruised by exhaustion—he answers questions about censorship and government meddling in his films. For his part, Zhang, forty-five years old and, along with Chen Kaige (*Farewell My Concubine*), one of the pillars of the so-called Fifth Generation of Chinese filmmakers, has never understood why his films get under the skin of government propaganda patrols. He considers himself a good Chinese citizen. Like the Chinese Communist officials, he is worried about the prospect of "chaos" if the increasingly toothless totalitarian state collapses too quickly. The specter of what has occurred in the former Soviet Union comforts no one here.

Like many intellectuals, he read the recent alarmist, futuristic book, *China Viewed Through a Third Eye*, which predicts anarchy as rural masses flood into the cities, seeking work and a piece of the action. He doesn't even object to the process of censors reviewing his films. He just feels they are wrong to ban them. In addition to *To Live*, two more of Zhang's films—*Ju Dou* and *Raise the Red Lantern*—were initially banned by authorities although later released after they collected dozens of international prizes. However, another of his films, *The Story of Qiu Ju*, was warmly embraced by the authorities and is said to have been viewed and approved by Chinese paramount leader Deng Xiaoping. Why the censors ban one film and praise another is a mystery to Zhang.

"I still feel very strongly that all my films are healthy and constructive," he said. Irritated that *To Live* was shown at last year's Cannes Film Festival without official permission from the Ministry of Radio, Film, and Television, the Chinese government in the fall issued strict new rules limiting foreign funding for Chinese movies unless officially approved. The new rules almost caused the cancellation of Zhang's latest project, a movie tentatively titled in English, *Shanghai Triad*, set in the corrupt and decadent Shanghai of the 1930s.

As usual in Zhang's movies, the film stars Gong Li. But in the middle of filming in Shanghai, Gong Li split with Zhang, reportedly for another man. It was another setback for a film already plagued by new rules and limited financing. To ensure that the movie would be made, Zhang was forced to enter into unwanted collaboration with the official Shanghai Film Studio. This marks a significant break in Chinese filmmaking. In the past, Fifth Generation directors such as Zhang, Chen Kaige, and Tian Zhuangzhuang (*The Blue Kite*) were able to make their films in relative freedom, only to run the gauntlet of censors later. "Now I feel more constrained," Zhang said. "I feel like I am being watched all the time."

But if Zhang feels the pressure, it doesn't show when he is on the set. Filming a scene here at dusk in the garden of the old Ruijin Vila that was once the residence of Nationalist leader Chiang Kai-shek, Zhang is very much in command. Whereas in his hotel room he appeared fragile and meek, on he set, his hands thrust deep into the pockets of his heavy, knee-length army surplus coat, Zhang is a picture of strength. He looks taller than his 5-foot-7 frame.

Several times he paces the concrete garden walk where the scene is set, making sure that the crew has wet the surface with a hose to give the effect of a recent rainfall. Several times he arranges the black-robed actors who are supposed to be gangsters guarding the entrance to the villa. Several times he instructs the driver of an antique truck how to approach the gate and swerve to the left at the last instant.

Two cameras are trained on the gate. A sense of purpose and artistry fills the garden. When he is sure every piece is in order, Zhang shouts into a battery-powered bullhorn. *"Kaishi,"* he yells to the truck driver, "Drive." Then when he sees the truck move he turns to the cameras. *"Shi Pai!"* he says—"Shoot!"

With this new movie, Zhang said optimistically in the hotel interview, he doesn't expect any trouble from government censors. "This film is not politically sensitive," he says assertively. Based on a recent popular novel by author Li Xiao and approved by the mainstream Shanghai studio, the film appears to meet the new conditions established by the government.

The movie is a period piece set in the 1930s, when the town was run by powerful gangsters such as "Big Ears" Du and "Pockmarked" Huang. Zhang says the main gangster in the movie is a composite of these two villains. Star Gong Li plays a Shanghai cabaret performer, a gangster's moll caught in a deadly love triangle with the head hood's handsome brother.

Chinese government censors approved the script because it depicts the wicked capitalistic past before Communist "liberation." In Zhang's talented hands, however, most viewers are likely to see a shocking similarity between the wicked past and the increasingly wicked present. "This film will have relevance for people living in today's China," Zhang said. "Guangzhou (Canton), Shenzhen, and Shanghai have a lot of similarities to those days."

Anyone who has visited China's major cities recently knows that prostitution, gambling, and organized crime are back. Atop the Rainbow Hotel in Shanghai, for example, is a dance club where hookers openly solicit Chinese and foreign customers. After the 1949 Communist victory, prostitution all but disappeared in China. Former prostitutes were sent to "re-education camps." But since 1978, when Deng Xiaoping liberalized the economy, the old vices have returned. A February report by the Public Security Ministry said that 288,000 people were arrested in 1994 on prostitution-related charges. Shanghai officials recently announced plans to crack down on drug- and sex-related crimes.

If Zhang Yimou does run into trouble with this new film as he has in the past, it will be because the 1930s decadence he depicts on the screen looks too much like today. People might be compelled to ask the one question the government does not want posed: "Why did we have the revolution?"

Although Zhang himself claims no political or social statement in his film, the irony of Shanghai's wicked past catching up with its socialist future pervades the set here. One recent afternoon, producer Wang Ganyi was wearing a sweatshirt the crew had printed up for the movie. Inscribed on the front was what amounted to a movie trailer for the new film: "What appears bad is not necessarily bad. What appears good is not necessarily good. The whole story takes place in what seems like the old Shanghai, but it is not just a story of old Shanghai. . . ."

The Extravagance and Simplicity of Zhang Yimou's Eye

CHOW SHUK-YIN/1995

FILMMAKING HAS ALWAYS HAD its own conventions, yet Zhang Yimou only wants to run counter to them. In his new film, *Shanghai Triad*, look for unconventional framing. He takes his camera lens back to the triad gangs of 1930s Shanghai, yet behind it all, he invites the spectator to look at a changing Chinese society.

Zhang Yimou was forbidden to attend the '94 Cannes Film Festival because *To Live* hadn't passed the Chinese film censors; this year, this Chinese director has become the figure everyone is awaiting. *Shanghai Triad* is formally competing as a Chinese film and is scheduled to be shown at Cannes on May 24th. On May 22nd, Zhang Yimou made his first appearance at the '95 Cannes Film Festival at the party of another competing film, *Good Men, Good Women*. When asked to comment on this film, he simply answered, "Very good, very moving"—it seems that Zhang Yimou and Hou Hsiao-Hsien are sympathetic toward one another.

Seeing Zhang Yimou receive such a welcome from foreign reporters and audiences at Cannes, I sense real hope for Chinese film. Hearing his words, one can imagine that in the next few years Chinese film could experience a great change.

I interviewed Zhang Yimou on a brightly sunlit day in Cannes. He seemed a bit tired, yet his flowered shirt rather suited the sunlight and beaches of southern France.

From *City Entertainment: Film Biweekly*, No. 421 (1 June 1995). Reprinted by permission. Translated by Stephanie Deboer.

This time, Shanghai Triad *didn't have any problems with the censors, did it?*
No, it didn't. China has already arranged to show it next month.

In Shanghai Triad, *you don't shoot a story about average people, but rather about* Shanghai Triad *gangs. Does this gangster film have any particular significance or reflect any kind of current societal or political situation?*
Actually, today's Chinese society has changed a lot. Many people have different ideas and aspirations, but quite a few think only about money and material possessions—urban people especially run after money and material things. The luxurious mansion and life in *Shanghai Triad* is connected with this change in China. Yet after they are sated with material goods, what is it that people need the most? The role of Shuisheng in the film represents something more pure and innocent.

Are you saying that Chinese people have already lost their purity and innocence?
At least some them have. Nowadays, many people only think about money; relationships among people are very utilitarian. Although this is a gangster film, it still doesn't exaggerate blood and violence. Many bloody and violent films have already been made. This time, in my use of child and female protagonists, I didn't want to glorify violence or the underworld but rather wanted to depict a childlike innocence and femininity that still remain in all this brutality. This is opposed to the typical gangster film—I didn't want to make another *Godfather.*

China's crime rate is incessantly rising. Filming a 1930s Shanghai triad or revenge film is inadequate to reflecting this situation.
I didn't directly reflect this reality; the rise in the crime rate is related to economic development and open door policies.

I've read that the actor for Shuisheng was chosen out of a hundred thousand middle school students. According to what criterion did you choose this actor, and what do you think about his performance?
I chose the two child actors for Shuisheng and A Qiao from one hundred who had already been picked by the assistant director out of a hundred thousand. I think that the eyes were the most important—what this boy seems to think when he looks at something. He's a child, right? And he has no acting experience and isn't able to carry out a performance on his own. When

shooting the film, I could only guide him—talk with him about the story, make him believe the story.

Gong Li plays the role of a singing girl this time, both entertaining and singing. How was her performance?
I'm very satisfied with her performance. Her role was very difficult to grasp—the inner feelings were quite layered and complicated.

I feel that the look of this old Li Baotian doesn't really resemble a triad boss but instead resembles a historical figure; he gives the vague impression of Chiang Kai-shek. Add to this the board over the mansion door that reads "Upright and Pure in Mind," and one begins to associate him with an emperor in the Forbidden City. This old Tang is an underworld emperor.
This old Tang *is* an underworld emperor.

At the end of the film, the boy looks at his surroundings while hanging upside down. Going with this inversion, could it be said that the entire underworld society is also turned upside down?
In the seven days that this boy spends in Shanghai after leaving his village, he sees so many revenge killings and retaliations that the whole world has certainly turned upside down for him.

You've said before that this boy looks at the triads of old Shanghai from the point of view of a spectator. At the very end, when he is brought back from the island to Shanghai, I would argue that he is no longer a spectator but rather is already involved in this brutal reality.
He *is* already involved. The things he's seen in these seven days are all likely to remain in his heart. After he's grown up would be another story.

All your films attach importance to color. What colors did you use this time to depict old Shanghai?
I wanted to convey a kind of luxurious atmosphere. So after talking it over with the cameraman and art director, we decided to use gold. In the section on the island, on the other hand, I wanted to express a kind of unsophisticated and natural feeling.

You worked with a French producer this time. Did they influence you in any way?
They all had real confidence in me—they were helpful, but didn't control

my ideas. They even provided suggestions for the costumes. Because Chinese people are unfamiliar with things like buttons and neckties for 1930s western clothing, they even found samples of western clothing from that period for us to look at.

Every time you make a film you always shoot themes with which you are familiar or have emotional ties. You aren't from Shanghai; how were you able to understand 1930s Shanghai and integrate it into the film?
History has already passed; we can only look at reference materials. Reading books and looking at pictures—these are our only sources of information.

Are there any directors you especially like, or any that have really influenced you? For example, Wong Kar-wai has said that Godard's influence on you has been great.
I've only seen a scattered selection of Western films. It isn't easy to see Western films in China. Moreover, I don't understand foreign languages. There are some films I've seen but then can't remember the details. No director has had any specific influence on me.

You will continue to make films that have political implications, won't you?
I'll just see what happens—I'll make what I can make. What's most important is shooting themes I personally like.

Everyone has taken notice of the fact that China is a huge film market.
Yes. China certainly is a huge market, but it's still developing. For example, last year there were two Western films, *Fugitive* and *True Lies*, that drew very large domestic audiences. Chinese people really like to watch Hollywood films. Recently, the Chinese government has approved the importation of ten Western films every year. This has had a great impact because Western films weren't imported at all in the past. I would say that in the short term, Chinese people could be drawn to Western films and Hollywood movies could take over the market. But speaking in the long term, the market could still return to Chinese film. Directors in China are all fairly anxious and want to preserve their status as directors.

Zhang Yimou: Only Possible Work Environment Is China

RENEE SCHOOF/1995

CHINA'S TOP DIRECTOR SAYS nothing—not fame abroad nor censorship at home—could make him shoot movies anywhere but China. "I definitely have to stay in China. This is where I live, where I'm familiar with everything, where all my personal experiences have been," said Zhang Yimou, the director of the Academy Award-nominated films *Ju Dou* and *Raise the Red Lantern.*

His latest movie, *Shanghai Triad*, a gangster tale starring Zhang's longtime leading lady Gong Li as a 1930's nightclub singer, opened the New York Film Festival on 29 September. But Zhang skipped the opening at Lincoln Center because, he says, he was pressured by the Chinese government. Festival organizers said Beijing was angry that an American documentary about the 1989 Tiananmen Square democracy movement—a film Zhang had nothing to do with—was on the festival program.

At a film festival sponsored by Robert Redford's Sundance Film Institute in Beijing this month, Zhang refused to go into particulars about missing the New York premiere. What is more important to him, he said, is how his film is received in China. "When I'm making a film I'm thinking form the perspective of what's in a Chinese person's mind, what does the audience see, what do they make of it," Zhang said in an interview. "I don't understand Western audiences—only very superficially. So it's hard to see from their perspective." Still there have been temptations to try. "More than one person

---

(5 November 1995). Reprinted by permission of The Associated Press.

has asked me to make a movie abroad," Zhang said with a laugh. "I could do it, but I couldn't make a good one."

Zhang at first modestly claimed he was not aware of what foreign critics say about his films because he does not speak foreign languages. But when pressed, he said he appreciates the warm reactions from audiences at international festivals. He was in Cannes in May for the opening of *Shanghai Triad.* "Naturally, as a director, I'm very happy that so many people pay attention to my films," he said in a quiet voice with a slightly sheepish smile.

Zhang is one of the critically acclaimed "Fifth Generation" of Chinese filmmakers, a small group who graduated from the Beijing Film Academy in 1984. His directorial debut, *Red Sorghum* in 1987, won the best-picture award at the 1988 Berlin Film Festival. *Raise the Red Lantern* and *Ju Dou* were banned in China, then later released. Zhang's *To Live*, winner of the Cannes Jury Grand Prix last year, still cannot be shown here [China]. The government was angry Zhang's partners submitted *To Live* to the Cannes Festival without its approval.

Despite other changes in the Chinese film world, censorship continues with no loosening in sight. "Everyone knows that in China you can't make whatever film you want. When we select our subject matter, there are limits imposed by the censors. That's the environment of our lives here," Zhang said. "We're used to it. I can still find a way to make movies."

At the same time, there are new problems. Now that most government subsidies have been withdrawn, filmmakers face the same problem as their counterparts in the West: money. Investors want good box-office receipts, so directors must appeal to audience tastes. Zhang's films are known for their beautiful cinematography and their exploration of human emotions under the pressures of life in China in a variety of settings. Some critics say Zhang and other Fifth Generation filmmakers, while appreciated abroad, are not as popular at home because Chinese moviegoers want action and foreign features, not artistic works about China's rural life and its past.

Yet Zhang, easily recognized by his gaunt face and crew cut, attracts crowds wherever he goes. Chinese know him as the son of blue-collar workers—someone without special privilege who made it big in the world's culture capitals. They are also fascinated by his longtime, now-ended romance with Gong. They made five movies since 1990 and split up during the filming of *Shanghai Triad* earlier this year. While several reporters interviewed Zhang outside the theater where the Sundance Film festival was held, a Chinese and

Western crowd gathered quietly, waiting for a chance to mob him for auto-
graphs. They were rewarded. Zhang paused to chat and scrawl his large signature on many festival programs.

Zhang is now working on a script about a subject he has never touched—
contemporary life in urban China. If all goes well, filming will begin later
this year or early next year, he said. "I always want to make different kinds
of films each time," he said. "That's the way to train, to become more resil-
ient. I want to try different styles."

Paving Chinese Film's Road to the World

LI ERWEI/1996

Collaborating with Writers

LI: *Which Chinese writers do you like?*

ZHANG: There are so many writers in China, and I like so many of them. I really like the writers with whom I've worked, such as Mo Yan, Liu Heng, Su Tong, and Wang Shuo. Their works could be called the literary parents of my films—even as they've displayed literary trends, they've also led trends in film. So if you want to see the development of Chinese film or the evolution of my own individual style, you can look to the future changes of writers.

L: *What do you think are the differences between the literary styles of Mo Yan and Chen Yuanbin?*

Z: Mo Yan emphasizes the creation of a world much in the same way as Gabriel García Márquez, while Chen Yuanbin is strictly realistic. I believe in being faithful to the spirit of the original and in drawing specific inspiration from it. I took from Mo Yan's *Red Sorghum* a kind of unrestrained, free, and detached mood, and then elaborated on it.

L: *If you were to compare* Red Sorghum *and* Ju Dou, *how would you say they differ? Why did you choose to adapt Liu Heng's* The Obsessed *at the time (1989)?*

Z: *Ju Dou* expresses a sense of repression. What moved me about Liu Heng's work was its absolutely unmerciful and unforgiving critique, as well as its

From *Living for Art, Not for Food*. Han Xiufeng and Xiao Hae, eds. Changsha: Hunan wenyi chubanshe (1996): 385–412. Translated by Stephanie Deboer.

Gong Li and Li Baotian, *Ju Dou*, 1989

Gong Li and Li Baotian, *Ju Dou*, 1989

He Saifei and Gong Li, *Raise the Red Lantern*, 1991

Gong Li, *Raise the Red Lantern*, 1991

Gong Li, *The Story of Qiu Ju*, 1992

Gong Li, *To Live*, 1994

To Live, 1994

Li Baotian, *Shanghai Triad*, 1995

Shanghai Triad, 1995

Wei Minzhi, *Not One Less*, 1999

Tian Zhenda and Wei Minzhi, *Not One Less*, 1999

Zhang directing schoolchildren, while Wei Minzhi stands behind him, *Not One Less*, 1999

penetrating portrayal of Chinese human nature. At the time, I'd been comparing *The Obsessed* and *Red Sorghum*. *Red Sorghum*'s unrestrained force of life and wild attitude toward living—its public display of unfettered human nature—was actually full of an ideal flavor rarely found in Chinese people, even contemporary Chinese people. But Liu Heng's *The Obsessed* is different—what he depicts is the actual mindset of real Chinese. Even though he writes historical fiction, it's still very realistic. It's this kind of realism in *The Obsessed* that deeply moved me. I felt that the characters of this work were actually Chinese—Yang Tianqing really is a typical Chinese. He has wicked designs but lacks the guts to act on them—every exterior movement makes him tremble with fear. His burden is extremely heavy, and his heart twisted and repressed. But at the same time, he's unable to control his instinctual impulses and desires. He's like a thin pancake fried in hot oil—fry both sides, and the result is that neither the inside nor the outside is a person. This Yang Tianqing is the perfect representative of the actual mindset of Chinese people. I really liked this at the time. I felt that this work was really forceful. At the same time, from another point of view, I felt that it allows us to see Yang Tianqing in our own reflections. If you say that *Red Sorghum* is written expressively, then *Ju Dou* is written repressively; if you say that what *Red Sorghum* displays is unlawfulness, then the established practices of *Ju Dou* force people into comers, even to the point of death. These rules are produced by the characters themselves and haven't been produced externally, so the characters themselves—and not society—also produce their own tragedy. If you were to take the "my grandpa" personality of *Red Sorghum* and place it onto Yang Tianqing, its tragedy could turn into a stirring ode. He could choke the old man to death and by the second day already sleep with Ju Dou. So all this is to say that *Red Sorghum* and *Ju Dou* express very different things.

L :   *I think that compared to* Red Sorghum, Ju Dou *was shot a bit more maturely. Its narrative is also a bit smoother.*

z :   [He smiles.] Of course, I was one or two years older! When I shot *Red Sorghum*, I was a fearless young calf. I liked that kind of unrestrained energy. I filmed it rather impudently, elaborating on the inherent quality of Mo Yan's work. But it's still quite lacking in terms of completeness and maturity.

What's valuable is its impudence, but its incompleteness and coarseness also makes this impudence seem a bit primitive.

L :   *You know Liu Heng very well—you're good friends. What opinion do you have of his works?*

z :   Liu Heng is one of those rarely seen writers with profound skill at depicting characters. His fiction, such as *Dongzhimen*, typically places its characters on the hot pan to fry, cooking their insides until they're no longer a person, on the inside nor the outside. Many of his characters are like this—it's really interesting. Actually, this is also an expression of something very strong in Liu Heng himself, and this is something that everyone has. Societal progress and industrial development have caused people to create a kind of psychological barrier or form a kind of pressure and conformity. Both the East and West have this. And life wants to break through this kind of thing—people instinctively want freedom and want to shout—so this forms struggle and conflict, producing uncountable stories that move us to tears. Liu Heng's works squarely face this. He truly adapts it into what he writes, and he writes about things that Chinese people usually don't dare face up to. Moreover, he doesn't write about ideas or external things, and he doesn't say that everyone's tragedy is a result of the Cultural Revolution, the politics of external movements, or of societal reasons. He looks for it in human beings themselves instead. This is an improvement, and it's what's most valuable in Liu Heng's works.

L :   *Everyone is interested in the question of the use of red in all your films, such as the red sorghum of* Red Sorghum, *the red-dyed cloth of* Ju Dou, *the red lanterns of* Raise the Red Lantern, *and the red peppers of* The Story of Qiu Ju. *Apart from the fact that red is full of expressive power and can strongly impact people's visual senses, is there some other reason for your liking red so much?*

z :   This is related to the fact that I'm from Shaanxi Province. Shaanxi's soil is rather red, and its people are fond of this color. All kinds of affairs held in the provinces of Shaanxi and Shanxi are likely to make use of the color red. Such customs have influenced me and have caused me to be fond of red. I then turn around and display this same color.

L :   *Looking back at your collaborations with writers again, what do you think directors should capture when adapting a work of literature to the screen?*

z :   I think that every work has its own spirit. A director must capture this spirit of the work, then take this spirit and emphasize it, amplify it. As for the filming of *Red Sorghum, Ju Dou, Raise the Red Lantern,* and *The Story of Qiu Ju,* I feel that my understandings of their original works were correct.

L :   *Of all the films you've directed, which is your favorite?*
z :   That's really hard so say. They're like your own children—you love them all. But comparatively speaking, I still like *Red Sorghum* because it was my first effort. I also like it because it's full of passion.

L :   *Beginning with* Red Sorghum, *all your protagonists have been women, among which Jiu'er, Qiu Ju, and Ju Dou are all women with expressive and unrestrained characters—only Songlian is a little oppressed.*
z :   I don't like that kind of oppressed, always tightly sealed woman very much. While Chinese people live very hard lives, they must always try to realize themselves in the face of oppression.

L :   *But your female protagonists are all women who face oppressive lives.*
z :   Writing about women facing oppression allows you to more effectively illustrate a problem because women endure a few more things. Traditionally speaking, it is perhaps a little easier for a man to accomplish something, yet it's more difficult for a woman. As for my films all having female protagonists, this is actually related to the fiction I've chosen. If you think about this in terms of the developments and changes in literature, you'll understand why I film women and why I film the countryside. If you talk about film from the perspective of cultural trends or the cultural mindset of writers, you'll understand this more thoroughly.

L :   *Do you discuss literature with writers?*
z :   [He smiles.] I've always discussed writers behind their backs—when they face me, I have nothing to say, and only talk about questions of artistic collaboration. When I first see someone's work, no words come to my mind. Fortunately, I now enjoy a bit of prestige. Writers are rather confident in me.

L :   *Gong Li has told me that you're arranging Wang Shuo's* I'm Your Father. *Why have you suddenly jumped from filming about rural themes to filming about urban ones?*

z :   I've always wanted to make a film about the city. I've just never found a suitable script.

L :   *So what kind of style do you intend to use to shoot this film?*
z :   I'm now still revising the script and trying to capture its feeling. Nothing's been determined regarding who will supply the money or how it will be filmed, so I don't want to say too much. Publicizing too early could put me in an awkward position. I've chosen this entirely new theme to force myself to vary my pattern. If I were to choose the same theme or the same type of theme, it would be difficult for me to change.

L :   *What impressions do you have of Wang Shuo?*
z :   The art resembles the artist. The minute you meet him, you really understand his works because those works are him. From laughter to cursing, all of life's attitudes are addressed in his works. *I'm Your Father* is, comparatively speaking, a rather serious work of his. Beyond this laughing and cursing, there's also a larger topic. This is what I see. If I'm to film it, I want to film it differently than his earlier works as much as possible. Many people have filmed his works in the past, but they've all been inferior to his original works. Wang Shuo is difficult to grasp. It's very hard to make your way out of his language and style. I'm now revising the script and have discovered one problem—it could very easily turn into his copy. If you're not even the slightest bit careful, it could turn into a copy of his work. If this is how it turns out, then I have no choice but to abandon the effort. The seductive power of Wang Shuo's work is strong—he leads you along despite yourself. Also, his control is formless. This illustrates how great his works are. He is, after all, the first writer in China to have commercial appeal, and this is a rare phenomenon. This guy is a hero of turbulent times. Some people say that his works lack any overall pattern. He's said to me, "I don't want to tire myself that way. A stream of witty remarks are amusing, but once they're finished, that's it." He doesn't want to write large works; he doesn't have that strong a sense of mission or historical responsibility. He doesn't want to paint a great picture, having some disdain for what's usually recognized as the great picture. His recent works repeat themselves, roll over themselves. But this way is also correct—it's quite Hollywood-like. Sell whatever sells well. It's great. Chinese writers also have a commercial awareness now, and this is inevitable in the development of a society.

How to Be a Film Director

L : *Ever since* Red Sorghum, *you've gone through many complications in your professional and home life. Have you changed in any way?*
z : There hasn't been any significant change. Over these past few years, I've always thought about how to be a good director and how to shoot my films well.

L : *I've heard that you're very amiable on location—that you rarely lose your temper.*
z : I rarely lose my temper on location. I feel that there's no need to curse people, scold people, or throw things on location. If everyone works hard and they truly intend to do well, then I feel there's no need to blame anyone if difficulties arrive for any objective reason. What you really need to do then is figure out how to resolve the difficulty. A director is the commanding officer of the shooting location and is perfectly justified in getting angry. But the more you actually realize this, the more you don't want to lose your temper. Some people think that you're not a director if you don't curse people, but I'm not so sure about this. Actually, everyone is equal on the shooting location. When a film is successful, the director is the one who receives the most fame and gain, regardless of whether or not you even care about this fame. The production team of several dozen to over a hundred people receives very little. They may come to your project in order to work with you as a director, or they may feel that your salaries are rather high or that your production team isn't bad. We see all these names appear on the screen, but who really pays attention to them? So you could say that they're donating to a cause. To use a Chinese analogy, they're the bearers of a sedan chair, and it's the director and actors who sit in that sedan chair. Of course, there are distinctions in the division of labor—it's like this all over the world. But speaking in terms of relationships among people, I feel that the director should be careful not to disappoint everyone's hard work. All the hard work of the production team rests on the shoulders of the director. Everything depends upon how the director grasps it, so he or she has to be diligent. Even if directors feel themselves to be the center of their production team—its master—if they film carelessly, then all the production team's hard work will flow through your hands like water. Even if you surround your director with the most outstanding people in the world and even if they exert one

hundred percent effort, if the director isn't careful the film will unmistakably fail. To tell the truth, I don't think this is easy for anyone. Regardless of the attitudes they bring to the production team, they all have to work hard with the director for so many months, each having his or her own difficulties. Thus, the director must enable everyone to live in harmony and maintain as much equality with everyone as possible when working.

L : *I've heard that you often practice what you preach with the production team and personally help out with such things as digging ditches. Do you feel that a director such as you who has achieved such success really needs to do this?*
z : You can't say that it's not necessary. Of course, people say that a director is an intellectual laborer, and they only want the director to design or think about the film. So as soon as you go to do something, everyone says, "Please don't worry about this, go and worry about the film. Hurry up and think about your film!" Many production team members will treat you this way. This kind of talk has become jargon to express their respect for the director. But actually, a director really isn't thinking about the film twenty-four hours a day; moreover, you can't just come up with something whenever you think about it. So I still help everyone out when I have the time. Even if you carry one brick to everyone else's ten, you're still conducting a kind of emotional communication, so I participate in whatever work I can. Actually, I've recently done this work less and less because other people often stop me. In the years when we made *Red Sorghum* and *Ju Dou*, I was really on the front lines, but now everyone places me on a pedestal. But I get a lot of satisfaction when I can stand alongside everyone and work.

Regarding Collaborative Films

L : *Except for* Red Sorghum, *your* Ju Dou, Raise the Red Lantern, The Story of Qiu Ju, *as well as the film in which you and Gong Li acted,* A Terracotta Warrior, *have all been made with foreign cooperation. One could say that you've accumulated much more experience in utilizing foreign capital and filming methods than other directors.*
z : Actually, it's very difficult to attract foreign capital to make a film. Foreign investors are very careful about where they put their money. If they allow you to make your art for yourself with their money, then they're crazy. They demand earnings when they contribute it. Our attracting foreign capital all depends upon our own particular value, and our works are

testimony of this value. Every director wants to have more capital, an even higher level of freedom, and more room in which to play. I'm no different. But if you want to realize these aspirations, then you have to make good films.

L : *Then what, in your opinion, makes for a good film?*
Z :   As for what kinds of films are good films, everybody can judge for themselves. In my opinion, good films should first be attractive. This kind of attractiveness includes satisfying the differing demands of different kinds of people so that those who want to watch excitement find it appealing, and those who want to see "ideas" also think it's OK. The second is that it should say something of substance. Everyone spends so much money to buy a movie ticket; you've got to have something worth seeing.

L : *What do you think are the prospects for Chinese collaborative films?*
Z :   This will depend on changes in the film system. Collaborative films are a normal occurrence overseas. China has already made steps toward this, and this will undoubtedly develop in the future. The prospects should be very good.

A Quiet and Solitary Personality

L : *The films you've recently made have been very successful and have had much influence overseas. What kind of reaction have your parents had to this?*
Z :   They're, of course, very happy. Older people, you know, always hope that their children will become great.

L : *Do you often go back to see them?*
Z :   I don't go back very often. I'm a little ashamed of this. Actually, I'm not even close to having fulfilled the duties of a son. I can only care for one thing at a time! Film is an art of motion, and filmmakers are also always moving. Our homes seem to be wherever we are. But as long as I make good films—even if I'm unable to attend to my family—any parent would be pleased to see that I'm successful in my undertakings. If I gave priority to being filial, then I couldn't attend to making films. I've spent the last four successive Chinese New Years overseas and really have no way of looking after my parents. I'm really thankful that my younger brother and sister-in-law are there to look after them.

L : *I've found that your personality is a little peculiar—you don't like social interaction. To be a director but not like social exchange, this could offend many people.*

z : I'm really not good at this. In this respect, directors like Chen Kaige and Wu Ziniu are all stronger than I am. Other directors all know to write people letters during holidays—send things like New Year's cards. I never think of it. Ever since I was small, I've always liked being quiet, liked being alone, and didn't like visiting other people. I always stay at home the first two days of the New Year. We have so many relatives in our family, but I haven't seen them for dozens of years. I also don't like to talk a lot. When I was a cinematographer, I rarely spoke. But now that I'm a director, I can't not speak, so my mouth has become a bit more agile through use. But as soon as I leave a film, I'm no good anymore.

L : *Was this personality of yours a product of your home environment?*

z : I don't know. This can't be rationally analyzed. This is how I was born. It's very easy to be misunderstood.

L : *You've told me once that you have type A blood. Perhaps your personality has something to do with your blood type.*

z : Maybe. I also know that my personality isn't good at interacting and communicating with other people. At one time, though, I became aware of this and tried hard to change. But after a while, I was still the same as I'd originally been. There's nothing you can do about how you were born. This kind of personality could easily cause misunderstandings with friends—especially those friends who've helped me—and thus influence evaluations of my character. Actually, I'm rather good to people. I'm not an evil person without good intentions toward others. I hope that friends can show a little understanding about this. And I hope that, after a while, they'll be fine once they've seen a new work of mine—this is a kind of communication.

"I Haven't Pandered to Foreigners"

L : *There are people who think that you make films for foreigners—that you pander to their tastes. Do you have any reaction to this?*

z : I've never agreed with this point of view. I remember discussing the question of how Chinese film should go into the world ten years ago. At that time, there were also people who had doubts about whether we should move toward the world. How have we come to today, where people's ideas still haven't changed—it's still all the same. Beginning from *Red Sorghum*, I've been accused of such things as filming only the dark or backward aspects of China. I don't think so. If you say that I make films for foreigners, then for which foreigner am I making it? There are just too many of them. There are over a hundred countries in the world, and there are different kinds of foreigners with different kinds of tastes. It isn't possible to pander to foreigners, as far as I know. For a person like me who doesn't understand even a sentence of a foreign language, who doesn't understand foreigners at all, and who doesn't know what they like or what they want to see, how should I film then? Who should I film it for? From first touching the script to shooting the few films I've directed, we've only considered the reception of Chinese audiences—how Chinese audiences might view this film—and have never wanted to pander to foreigners. You couldn't cater to international film festivals even if you wanted to. I've attended so many international film festivals and have also acted as a festival judge. I know that there can be dozens of judges at each film festival and that they change every year. So do you know who will be the judges this year? Do you know whose words will count? You've already begun making your film a year ago, so have you made it for the Italians, for the French, or for the Americans? As far as I know, the audiences of these countries have different tastes. Even if you wanted to cater to them, it would be very difficult to decide what to do. It's simply impossible. If a director made a film in this way, he or she would surely die of exhaustion.

L : *Moreover, film festival judges come from different countries. Most of them speak different languages and have different loves and interests.*

z :   As far as I know, every person who judges at a film festival must be a film director, an actor, a producer, or have some status in the film world. And people with even a little bit of status all have personality, are very self-aware, and could never be influenced by others. Moreover, they're often opposed to one another. When I was a judge at the Moscow Film Festival, all the judges sat around in a circle. Behind each judge stood an interpreter so that every time someone said something, each interpreter could translate it into his or her own language. With all these people with strong personalities and strong likes and dislikes, who could pander to whom? In other words, say you make

a film for the sake of a film festival; you know that this year's festival likes
the color blue, so you film blue. But then the judges could be changed with
the next judges liking green. So you have absolutely no way of catering to
their tastes. It's best to just forget this idea. At the same time, there's no
reason to do all this, either. As long as you shoot a truly good film, everyone
will like it—it doesn't matter if it's a Chinese or foreign audience. In China,
anyone who reaches a certain level will receive this kind of accusation, and
I've received it many times on the mainland. I often say, "You say that I
pander to foreigners. Well, why don't you try to cater to them? First tell me
what foreigners like. First tell me what kind of film can win an international
award. You first give it a try." You'll soon discover that it's useless to do this.
This isn't the right way to make a film.

L :   *As for the question of focusing on the ignorant and backward aspects of China,*
have foreign audiences mentioned this at all?
z :   I feel that it's close-minded to say that foreigners enjoy seeing our
ignorance and backwardness or to say that foreigners are making fools of us.
This is an example of people not having confidence in themselves, of having
prejudice against their own things—you could even call it a provincially-
minded reaction. We don't enjoy the fact that Chinese film has won awards
overseas but rather say that this is an example of foreigners intentionally
making fools of us. This mentality is so ridiculous. Among all the Westerners
with whom I've come into contact, there hasn't been one person who's said
anything like, "You Chinese are ignorant and backward," or said, "Your life
is harder than ours." Not one person. Film festival judges are world famous
film artists—they're masters of their professions. Not only have they not
spoken to me in this way, the many ordinary Western audience members
who ask me all kinds of questions have also never mentioned these
things—not even once. This is what I know from my experience: I don't
intend to exhibit the ignorant and backward aspects of China, and no one
has regarded you in this way.

L :   *What do you think is the reason for these discussions to appear domestically?*
Besides not understanding the state of world film or the circumstances surrounding
film festival selection—even adding the provincial close-mindedness of certain
people—do you think there might any other reason?

z :   Their saying these things might be due to the fact that my last few films weren't able to be shown publicly right away. Many Chinese people couldn't see them, thus arousing many people's conjecture and comment. One other point might be that the strong expression of national culture in my films in combination with foreign praise of them might have caused people to mistakenly think that I was pandering to foreigners. Actually, the Westerners able to do a little criticism of Chinese film all like China and study China. They're foreigners interested in Chinese culture. Their tastes are similar to that of Chinese audiences, and they often speak the same language as you. You can't treat these people as real or typical Westerners. There's no way for you to understand what a true Westerner likes.

"I Want To Bring Chinese Film to the World"

L :   *Having attended so many first-rate international film festivals, what are your impressions of theme?*

z :   Going to a film festival is like going to a country fair. [He laughs.] Everyone meets, they exchange a few amenities, and that's it. People bring films there to exhibit as well as to sell. To phrase it pleasantly, it's a cultural exchange; to phrase it more commonly, it's simply a meeting of material exchange. I go to film festivals with two goals in mind. The first is to watch films and the second is to interact with friends.

L :   *Are you and Gong Li often surrounded by people at film festivals?*

z :   No. This happens much less frequently than in China because there are so many kinds of people there and too many people for them to surround. We're minorities at film festivals. [He laughs.] The people who are really encircled are all those big Hollywood stars. I watch as many films as possible when I'm at film festivals because we often aren't able to see world films in China when they're released. Film creators unable to see the world's newest, most popular films right away have no way of understanding the world and no way of reexamining themselves. This is really regrettable. If you rely on collecting your own material or viewing them when there's a retrospective, you'll have to wait until many years later. You'll lag behind. So all I can do is use my opportunities to leave the country to see them.

L :   *You've had so many opportunities to leave the country and always go to big film festivals with good films. We should say that your understanding of world film is somewhat greater than that of other directors.*

z : I wouldn't dare to say that. Actually, I still see too few films. I don't think that anyone can really grasp the developments or trends of world film. Those who do theory might be able to summarize and forecast this, but I don't dare let myself talk nonsense by saying that Chinese or world film is in this or that trend. Because you're mainly engaged in creating films—you're busy all year round with it—you can't come back and say that you understand world cinema just because you've managed to see eight or ten films. That's just too farfetched; it's too ridiculous. What you understand of world film is only a small part of the whole; you don't understand the whole at all, so how can you come up with foresighted criticism? At the same time, you also can't align yourself too closely to them or use them as guidelines for your own filmmaking. I feel that this simply shouldn't be done. So we should still persist in our own basic ideas. You can't look to other people's things to influence you. But those who study theory may be able to summarize the development of world film after they've seen a great amount of modern film and studied a great amount of material.

L : *Do you think that Chinese film, Chinese directors, actors, and other creative artists should attend film festivals and film exchanges more often?*
z :   This is absolutely essential. Attending international film festivals, receiving awards, and participating in all kinds of international activities—all of this is necessary. Because film is propagated very quickly and because it's a exceedingly wide-ranging artistic form, it can help people to understand our nation, culture, and living conditions. There are a few hundred film festivals in the world, and I think that they're all cultural stages. Since they're stages and since people from all over the world make appearances there, then Chinese people should also appear among them. Regardless of whether they're from mainland China, Hong Kong, or Taiwan, Chinese people should all step onto the stage. Each time we step onto this stage and make an appearance, then people can see that "there is China" and "this is Chinese film." Despite the fact that receiving an award isn't easy—people certainly won't give you an award lightly because the competition is so tough—we still should make an appearance and pursue an award. This has the same meaning as attending the Olympics and getting the gold medal. We have to distribute films, and we have to attend film festivals and introduce ourselves—display our own culture and national character. We must face the world and fight for more people to recognize

and have interest in our film products. Let the world see that there is a China, that there is Chinese film.

L :   *Before attending the forty-ninth Venice Film Festival with Gong Li, did you predict the competitive strength of* The Story of Qiu Ju?

z :   I've attended many film festivals, and I've never been willing to do much forecasting about whether or not I'd win an award. I know very clearly that this is a waste of energy and torment. No one can predict this. This particular film festival invited me to be a judge, but I gave up the right to be one so that *Qiu Ju* could be judged impartially.

L :   *As far as you know, what kind of position does Chinese film hold in the world now?*

z :   Of course we're still weak—there's no doubt about that. There's no need to talk about commercial films because as we used to say, "America is the number one enemy of the people of the world." [He laughs.] Hollywood films dominate the markets of every country you go to. There's no way around it. If you put aside commercial films and simply talk about so-called "art films," we also occupy a weak position because there are too few good films. You can't let America only know about one Zhang Yimou. If you really want to infiltrate their markets, you have to have a big group of people and a huge pile of works. And it also has to come in a steady stream, year after year. The kind of gasps of breath we have now is no good.

L :   *Why do you think Chinese film is unable to move toward the world? Where lies the problem? Is it that we don't have people of talent? That our ideas are out of date? Our techniques lagging behind? Or is it a production problem?*

z :   There are many problems. And the result of all these problems is that we have too few good films. We mustn't think too highly of ourselves. China has very good directors and actors, and our artistic talent isn't inferior to anyone else—this I acknowledge—but we still haven't presented even a few good films. You might dare to say that ten first-rate films are exported out every year. They must have real influence and must be really great. But actually, many people choose to go to movies based on the opinions of others. As long as everyone says it's good, then this good impression will lead other people to imperceptibly accept it. Why do so many people understand foreign stars so well? Why is it that mainland youngsters will say that Hollywood stars are as familiar as old friends, yet know nothing about our own actors? In all this, of course, lies the problem of incompetent advertising, but the main problem still is that there aren't very many good works or good stars. They aren't able to generate that kind of influence. If you want to produce good films, you have to be made of iron yourself. Only when there are good works will there be good prospects or a good situation. If there are no good works, then any display of pride is useless. It's no good to blindly think you're great. Of course, everyone treats you coldly or doesn't understand you, but there's still nothing for you to be angry about. To tell the truth, I used to really love getting angry. I know so many American films, yet they don't know anything about even one of our films, which made me want to fight. But I later came to feel that there's no need to get angry because we really don't present many good works. Our foundation is very shallow. We rely on our own resources, and we won't be able to come up with the money. So Chinese film still has a long way to go; there's still an arduous road to walk.

L :   *If the film system were changed, what do you think would happen to Chinese film?*

z :   If film policies were relaxed in the future and if free distribution were permitted, American film would definitely threaten our national film at first. This isn't true only of American film; all those Hong Kong films would also come to strangle you. Russian film is now being crushed by American film, but this is all temporary. Wait until your film renews itself again, and it'll be able to pass the stiffest test.

L :   *Do you think that there are still new paths to take in terms of film expression and technique?*

z :   Over the development of film up to today, techniques such as long shot and montage have all been used, and world film techniques have all stabilized. Its like martial arts—every path has already been traveled. No one can come up with styles that shock everyone any more; it isn't possible. You can't come up with anything new because the times for blazing new trails and ideas have already passed. You can only use the techniques already available to film, so in this respect you don't go and look for any new devices because there aren't any there. But new techniques could still emerge in film because film and industry, science and technology are all closely related. Any

big technological breakthrough could cause significant changes in anything
from film production to film viewing and showing. That's when a new film
language could be produced. But for now, with no significant breakthroughs
in technology, you tend to use those few stable methods such as long shot
and close shot. Although people are now saying that MTV and commercial
advertising have brought something new to film, film technique basically
hasn't changed. What continues to draw audiences nowadays is still the
depiction of people—stories about people and their fate. It's just that all
kinds of effort, craftsmanship, and technique are done to support these
stories.

L : *Your films have already had a certain influence in the world, so you could say
that your prospects look pretty good.*
z : I seem to have good prospects, but I also know that I still live in a very
difficult time period. I still hope to maintain the freedom to do as I
wish—just film whatever I'm interested in. I hope to continuously
change—not have any fixed style—and on the whole do every style solidly
and thoroughly. Each style has its own strengths and weaknesses, so we'll
always face different problems, but we can never be caught in between styles.

L : *When will you film* Peach Blossom*?*
z : *Peach Blossom* will probably have to be put aside first because I have to
revise the script. Also, it wouldn't be finished in time for the season if I filmed
it now. So we'll put it aside for a while.

L : *You and your generation of directors were on the vanguard of bringing Chinese
film into the world; everyone knows this clearly.*
z : Actually, we haven't had the effect of a vanguard movement. I feel that
what we've actually done is pave the road toward it. There was no possibility
for the commercial films of our generation to infiltrate foreign markets.
What my classmates, generation mates, and I were able to accomplish was
nothing more than allowing the world to begin to recognize us, as well as
begin to understand Chinese film. We now occupy a small and weak
position. We really can't rely upon one or two directors and a few works to
establish Chinese film's world image. We can only be the pavers of the road
for Chinese film, and the hope of Chinese film rests on young people—the
efforts of a younger generation. In twenty years, they should be able to open

international prospects with an even stronger image. Our greater prospects lie in the future.

[Zhang Yimou has begun shooting his new film, *Keep Cool*, in Beijing. Just as he was putting together this new film, Zhang Yimou and the writer met a number of times to continue several long talks in a Beijing teahouse.]

"I Know Myself Rather Well"

L : *Domestically, there are a few critics who think that you're on a downward slope—that your time has already passed. Do you have any opinion about this evaluation?*

z : I'm just a film director who ardently loves film and hopes to make it a life-long profession. I don't think that my films are so great as to become a representative of the times—at best it's just a particular moment. It's just that many people see and discuss my films. So whenever I see domestic critics fixedly summarizing my work according to certain trends and idealisms, I think that they're missing the point a bit. I always reflect on a film after finishing it. In fact, I've already conducted a very critical self-examination and summary earlier on. More often than not, once a film has been completed, I'm as familiar with it as my own child; I know all its strengths and weaknesses. When this child walks into the crowd, everyone goes to see and evaluate it. I normally don't say very much, but in my heart I know exactly how things stand. This is probably my strong point. I've never thought of myself as that extraordinary, and I've never thought that because a certain film didn't fulfill my expectations that I'd be on a downward slope from then on or from then on see the end of my talent. I know myself rather well and rather objectively. So, often before any of our films come out, we creative workers have already objectively appraised it. We're all rather good at reflection and are able to maintain a critical view of things. Filmmakers are very clear about this because it's very difficult to make a film in China.

L : *I've heard that since* Shanghai Triad, *you're demands for scripts have become even higher.*

z : But this didn't begin with *Shanghai Triad*, but rather—I think—started during a low period in Chinese literature. I had no choice but to spend even more time on the script. Literature is the parent of film. When literature isn't flourishing, then the standard of the scripts from which we directors must choose isn't as high as in the past. So this time I planned to make the next script a little more solid. One other point about filming so-called contemporary themes is that I also want to film something I've never shot before, at least as much as I can. I hope that for each film I make, I've never filmed it before—that they're fresh for me, at the very least.

"I'm No Stranger to the City"

L : *If you were to film the city, what kind of city would you have on your mind?*

Z : Everyone has their own different ideas of the city. It makes no sense for those of us who live in the city to feel like strangers in it. Everyone says that I'm an expert at filming rural themes. In fact, I only worked on a production team for three years; I didn't live in the countryside for very long. Our notions of the peasantry sometimes just come from our own experiences. It would be very difficult to have the opportunity again to live closely with them for a long period of time today. Instead, the scope of our lives today is concentrated in the city—our human experiences all stem from it. Because of the success of my past few films, everyone stubbornly clings to the idea that I can only film rural themes. I think that this point of view is a bit rootless. I think that you shouldn't look at anyone in a fixed way. I never take a fixed view of any director today. When you talk about works, you can discuss their success or failure, but don't put them in a box. Today's society is multifarious, and traces of the city have become more and more marked on all of us growing up in urban environments, so it makes no sense to be unfamiliar with it. But having said this, what each person is familiar with is simply a part of him- or herself. City life is different from life in the countryside. Rural life is one big atmosphere, and general conditions are all about the same. Because the city is intensely pluralistic, everyone has different points of view due to differences in type, class, identity, and profession. This is pluralism; its variables are great. Each person's part of the city is part of his or her character; it's their own point of view. Thus, we can't take a film with a contemporary urban theme and say to everyone, "OK, your representative city has arrived!" You can't say this. No one can say, "My city film represents a particular time period." Fewer and fewer people can represent the modern period because the city is increasingly personified, individualized, and plural. So I don't have so much ambition when I prepare to film my understanding of the city. I just want to depict a particular condition of contemporary people. I often see critical articles with tones that

I feel are much too big. Our manner of speaking about film—especially contemporary urban films—is all too big. When we study contemporary people and their spirit today, and when we look at the works of young, middle-aged, or older directors, it should all depend on each director's extremely individual point of view. I feel that we should never use such phrases as "fifth generation" or "sixth generation"; we should never base our analysis and view of works on the vision of particular generation. Each has always had his or her own look, so it's very strange that people persist in speaking this way. This kind of viewpoint is just blind, stupid stubbornness. Wanting to talk about the formation of a "fifth generation" is rather strange—what general character do they all share? I think that this generation was merely similar at the very beginning to some extent. This was a result of history. Similar societal experiences caused them to have a certain kind of commonality. But this so-called "common character" disappeared very quickly. So I've always believed that creative works have an individual character. We should look at individuality, and we should look to it even more in the future. I feel that the works of young directors, works of Jiang Wen for example, have become more and more personalized—this has also been determined by today's historical conditions. So I don't use such fixed aesthetic views as "fifth generation" to evaluate new works of today; this is wrong. What we can do is discuss works and look at their effects—how they effect every person today—from an individual perspective.

"The Key is to Film People"

L : *If you make a city film, will you pay close attention to the surface of the city, to the feeling of the city, or to something else?*
z : Displaying modernity is the same as displaying antiques. All these things become unimportant when you put your sights on people, when you truly begin to penetrate the spiritual world of people. When you make a film, the packaging becomes part of the story—part of the narrative—but it doesn't represent it. Relying on its wrapping and mold to establish yourself should be a thing of the past. Up to today, I've made eight films. But whenever someone talks about my films and still lingers on a fixed point of view—on things like "false folk customs" or "exhibiting antiques"—then they seem too out of date. Their point of view hasn't advanced theoretically at all. Regardless of whether the intent of these articles is to praise or destroy, they're all meaningless. And when this becomes the measure for evaluating

my new films, they're even more meaningless. The setting of a film—no matter if it's yellow earth or a five star hotel—if the story requires it, you just go film it. When its no longer required, nothing will fit. The pure image can't support the life of a film anymore because we've all become more advanced, including the audience. People today have so many different lifestyles. You can't say that it isn't right for people to film rock and roll, dance halls, or hooligans; they're also a part of city life. The key depends upon whether you've made it interesting or not. Does filming courtyard houses, narrow alleyways, carts, or big tea bowls always mean that you've made a film with Chinese urban characteristics? So does filming hooligans, rock and roll, and dance halls always reflect the vanguard spirit of city films? I'm afraid it isn't that simple.

L : *I've heard that there are some Western critics who don't really acknowledge Chinese urban themes. They think that city films aren't films with Chinese characteristics. This is a very strange point of view.*
z : It isn't strange—they've just never seen any good ones. If they'd seen good ones—seen many good ones—then they wouldn't think this way. Don't blame others; we should blame ourselves for not having filmed something good. It's also true that our most well received international film successes to date have mainly lain within the limits of "antiques" and the "countryside." Foreigners can see one or two films like this every year, and of course they're deeply impressed by them. But actually, China makes many films with contemporary themes every year, but few of them are made well, so foreign audiences aren't able to see them. If these films can't take part in film festivals, then no one will buy them for distribution, and then they can't see them.

L : *In your opinion, when Chinese filmmakers create films, how should they deal with contradictions between the aesthetic habits of foreign audiences and our creative needs?*
z : We can't determine the direction of our own filmmaking according to their aesthetic habits. This is out of the question. Films are made to be shown to audiences, not to a particular film critic or film festival. I think this is a question of common sense. If we had several extremely outstanding urban films every year to present to audiences (including foreign audiences), this would certainly influence their aesthetic habits. There's also a historical

reason. Chinese cultural history is age-old, and when Westerners travel to China, they all want to see these kinds of things, so they have certain expectations. Westerners' ideas can be changed, but the change will be slow. You can't have the achievements of five thousand years in front of you, and then expect them to suddenly like your contemporary things, especially since it was the West from which modern culture developed. There's no sense of freshness for them from the very beginning. So every change needs time.

"Express Your Own Uniqueness in Urban Films"

L : *A number of city films appeared in France that paid close attention to people's inner states—to the kinds of inner splits they face within an industrialized society. Do you think this kind of film could appear in China?*

z : Any kind of film could emerge in China; we can't use a fixed line of vision to look at the present state of Chinese film. I think that the present state of Chinese film can't be summarized by such words as "flourishing" or "lively" but is rather as a kind of change and development in the face of great difficulty. Any kind of film could appear in China. Anything could appear or not appear, and anything could succeed or fail. We should no longer use a fixed line of vision to look at things. So although I can't come up with a theory, I just feel that when I make films I should preserve what I consider to be my own particular character as much as possible. Regardless of the theme, this is all I can do because there are many difficulties that I personally can't overcome.

"I'm Just an Ordinary Person"

L : *You've already received great success. How do you evaluate yourself?*

z : As a director, I hope to be able to preserve a little uniqueness as long as possible, but this is really difficult to do. Up till now, I've never dared to imagine that I could have created anything great. Up till now, I've still felt myself to be an ordinary person, an average person. I've never found myself to have any element of genius. And I haven't yet found a true genius among our generation—someone whose creativity leads far ahead, causes us all to be amazed and filled with admiration or inspires the times. Actually, everyone is still rolling around in a circle. Sometimes you do well, and sometimes someone else does well. The lines of *Old Well* say, "Every third generation produces a man; every tenth generation produces a god." This so-called "god," of course, refers to a creative genius. From this, it's clear that peasants see very accurately. I've always felt myself to be an ordinary person, an average person. I have the good fortune to be engaged in this profession, and I have the good fortune to be doing what I like to do. It's in this respect that I'm much more fortunate than many people my age. It's not easy to be able to dedicate yourself to something in which you're interested. This is fate, and I'm content with my lot. Whenever I make a film, I'll often run into some difficult problem. At this time, I'll feel like an idiot who's never learned the skills necessary to the task. Then I'll often imagine, "If another person were to stand in my place and if that person were a genius, he or she would think of a way to solve this right now. This person would use some unique method to deal with this, and who knows how many times better than me he or she would be." Then I'll often imagine how I might desperately try to reach for that genius's idea, but it's a pity—in the end I'm still myself. So every one of my films has many shortcomings. Every single director knows that whenever you make a film, you'll always run into some very difficult problems—even blind spots—that your own abilities and boundaries will have no way of overcoming. This moment is often the most agonizing. Therefore, I'm in no way some kind of "rare talent," and I'm not one of those people who can make their way through any situation. A good film is actually the crystallization of many people's efforts. A director isn't particularly extraordinary.

L : *You really impress people with your ideas. Don't you feel that you do?*
z : No. If I were a genius who surpassed the IQ of all my colleagues, my films would be extraordinary. Unfortunately, I'm too average an ordinary person. In my artistic field, there are many great masters whose creations we still enjoy without limits, with whom many of us of later generations can't even compare.

L : *For example, you most admire . . .*
z : The music world, the art world—there are so many here. Beethoven, Mozart, Van Gogh—so many remarkable artists. They died young, yet they left behind so many outstanding works, and later generations couldn't surpass them. I believe that they were geniuses. To be honest, I feel that probably only God knows the proportion of genius to environment that produced them; their numbers are really limited. Whenever I make a film, I

feel that I'm not even close to being a genius and feel more and more at a loss of what to do. Every once in a while, when a film is completed and everyone thinks it's good, only I actually know that it would have been much better if a particularly great person had dealt with it. This genius would definitely have better "moves" and methods and could have achieved a much better effect! This genius is definitely out there somewhere—it's just that we haven't seen it because a film can have only one outcome! You'll never know whether other plans would have worked or not. You'll never know whether or not you chose the best ones because that would require a huge amount of talent and financial resources. Initially, you may be allowed many, many choices, but once you've decided on one choice, you need a great amount of labor power and material resources to complete it. And what you see is the only possible outcome of your choice. You'll never know whether or not what you've chosen is correct in the end because you've never seen the possibility of other choices—they haven't been produced. This is different from music and painting. For music and painting, you can paint three or four versions over the same base and then see all your choices. There's no way to see your choices in film. In many cases, you can only move in one direction. For every shot or scene, we can't shoot according to two plans without holding up the schedule or funds; this rarely happens. There's no way you could shoot two films at the same time and compare them. You shoot one section of the film, and you've already spent from several million to ten million, and it just gets more and more expensive. As a director, I often examine my own conscience: "Are you filming to the best effect? Is this the best choice?" And often I think, "I'm sure there's a better plan than this; it's just that I don't have the ability to find or execute it." I have no way of reaching the other shore. So how do you go about comparing and choosing? I'll often feel very dissatisfied. Sometimes, after a film is finished, everyone will say it's good, but I'll still know that this isn't the best it could be. Somewhere out there there's something that is. So from this perspective, the distance between genius and us is too far, and because of this we shouldn't casually place such words as "genius" or "rare talent" on people. Against all of human history, we're too insignificant. Over tens of millions of years of humanity, how many truly outstanding geniuses have left behind how much for us to enjoy? How can we compare with them? I'm extremely practical. I myself feel that I'm one of those slow types who needs to start early. I'm much older than all my classmates, and when I began school, I knew that that time was comparatively precious for me and that opportunities could be very difficult for me to obtain. So I didn't want to waste my time and worked hard to do well at what I love. I knew very clearly that I could only make a little over ten films in the rest of my life. My only hope was just to make every film—or at the very least make half of them—well. This was the only thing I could accomplish. If our films have attracted some attention from the outer film world, I hope that this attention will gradually broaden and cause the world to notice all the films of China and notice our younger directors to some extent. There's probably still a long way to go before Chinese film is truly powerful and prosperous. We're doomed to be a group of pavers who will lead national film over a long journey toward a brilliant future. This is probably where our so-called responsibility lies.

"Film Shouldn't Be Infatuated with Itself"

L :   *Beginning from the first film you directed,* Red Sorghum, *you've always paid attention to and demanded that you make your films as attractive as possible. You seem to be a director who really pays attention to the entertaining and enjoyment aspects of film.*

z :   That's right. Entertainment is a point upon which I always insist when making films. Film must definitely be made attractive—everything must be packaged in this attractiveness—yet it shouldn't indulge in self-admiration or that kind of self-infatuation that's distant from everyone. But what we're calling "entertainment" is still different from big commercial Hollywood films. What we make could still be considered artistic films. The films I make are all rather realistic, yet I still took for particular distinguishing features for every film. Each film is only a phase; I never want to repeat myself. My next film will likely be very different from my earlier rural films. I don't think that summaries that describe the "itinerary" or "direction" of a person's works are very accurate. If there's a direction, then there has to be a kind of destination—something to be persevered. For me, this is obviously not the case. I tend to choose themes as I like. This "doing as I please" is to maintain a kind of flexibility. I've never wanted to carry out many rational plans. Another point is that I have one principle in choosing projects—that I will be different than in the past. I really don't think about whether this film is commercial or artistic very much. I don't think about my future direction very much. I don't think about whether I'm a complicated kind of film director or a popular type of director. I also don't really think about plans for myself. As long as I feel that the film I'm making now is different from past films, then I'll make it. If it seems interesting, then I'll film it, and when its finished, it is finished. The next time I'll make something else. So there's no fixed itinerary to my filmmaking.

The Personal Is Political for a Chinese Director

DAVID STERRITT/1996

W HEN MOVIES ARE AT issue, China's government has a remarkable talent for embarrassing itself in public. And the country's most renowned filmmaker, Zhang Yimou, is often the figure at the center of the
storm. The most recent incident was touched off when Zhang's old-
fashioned mobster epic, *Shanghai Triad*, was selected by the New York Film
Festival for its coveted opening-night slot. Angered by the presence of a completely unrelated movie in the festival—a documentary called *The Gate of
Heavenly Peace*, about China's democracy movement—the Chinese authorities revoked permission for Mr. Zhang to attend the gala screening of his
film. The result: more press coverage for *Shanghai Triad*, for Zhang himself,
and for the documentary, that would ever have happened otherwise.

Something similar happened when China kept Zhang from the Cannes
Film Festival two years ago. His drama *To Live* was being honored with a slot
in the official competition, irking authorities who found the movie too critical in its view of recent Chinese history. A press conference for the director
went forward as planned—with a conspicuously empty seat at center stage,
reminding the world that a towering artist would have been present if not
for governmental petulance. *To Live* is still unreleased in China.

And fans in the United States still remember when Chinese authorities
tried to have Zhang's brilliant *Ju Dou* yanked from the Academy Award race

simply because the film's sardonic melodrama struck them as too downbeat for international consumption.

Zhang didn't make it to New York in 1995, but he did make it to Cannes in May, and I seized the opportunity to continue an intermittent dialogue I've had with him since our first meeting eight years ago. Meeting with a handful of journalists on a sunny balcony of the Grand Hotel, he proved as outgoing and articulate as ever.

Unlike most of Zhang's previous pictures, beginning with the rowdy *Red Sorghum* and continuing through works like the elegant *Raise the Red Lantern* and the ironic *Story of Qiu Ju*, the new *Shanghai Triad* is a straightforward genre piece with few subtexts or complexities. Set in Shanghai during the 1930s, it centers on a teenage boy who becomes the servant of a "Godfather"-type crime boss and his mistress, a brassy cabaret singer. "There's not much politics in this film," Zhang acknowledged through an interpreter. "To be honest, after the *To Live* incident, I am a bit tired."

Still, the picture does make implicit comments on the current state of Chinese life through its portrait of Shanghai's excesses some sixty years ago. "In its depiction of the world the boy enters—in terms of how materialistic society has become and how this influences people's views of money and [their] chase after material goods and how this affects human relations. . . . If you go to China today and talk to people, they'll be telling you [only] how they want to make money and improve their livelihoods. We want to convey that in the movie."

To carry this message, Zhang selected the "Godfather" genre rather than a format that might appear more neutral. The choice suggests that his views of current Chinese trends are not optimistic, and his conversation bears this out. "I think the country will become more and more materialistic," he says. "We're heading in that direction. I'm interested in asking the question: As our livelihood improves, how can we maintain our more human side? From this point of view, one can say [the film] is somewhat more political."

Another timely issue raised by *Shanghai Triad* is that of violence—on the screen and in the world. "In the 2000 years of [Chinese] history," Zhang says when asked about this, "there are many cruel tales of violence. It doesn't exist just today or in the last 1000 years. In the vision of [former Chinese leader Mao Zedong], violence is normal. . . . Power struggle [in China] has been a normal way of power transition to eliminate the enemy physically. In today's Chinese cities, this question keeps popping up whether to eliminate one's enemy physically."

All of which has led Zhang to a strong reaction against violence in his life and work, including *Shanghai Triad*, which contains some mayhem but treats it with more restraint than one finds in typical Hollywood productions. "I am someone who abhors violence," he says with conviction. "There's not much gangster violence in my own experience, but as I was growing up there was a lot of violence connected with politics . . . which turned family members against each other. I saw people beaten up for political reasons, and my family has repeatedly been struggled against. All this made an impression on me. . . . I keep thinking about why violence exists in such a way, to tear people apart." Zhang is also fascinated by the stories he's heard about real mobsters of the 1920s and '30s, whose activities went beyond the realm of crime and into the political arena. "My intention in the film is not to depict organized crime coming to China," he explains, "or how violence exists in gangster movies. I'm interested in violence and human relations—how violence affects the humanity behind the characters."

These thoughts helped motivate Zhang's treatment of the gangster's girlfriend. She enjoys a superficially easy life but knows that she can't trust any of the dangerous men who hover around her. Eventually she confides in a woman she meets when the gang is in hiding, and she starts to grow closer to the young boy at the center of the story. "They're not from the same class position," Zhang notes, "but there's the beginning of a relationship between them. What my movie wants to say is that it's important to build up understanding between people, to get rid of hostility and opposition."

If such understandings do come about and flourish, the result would be an improvement in Chinese life. "I think the Chinese people have been thinking about this issue," Zhang says of social conflict and violence, "and are heading toward a more liberal answer. I think China will take some time to become a more liberal society, however, and it won't be as simple as Westerner's might think because [the nation] is carrying a big [historical] burden."

The character of the girlfriend is played by Gong Li, who has starred in all of Zhang's major films. She was also widely praised in 1993 for her work in the popular *Farewell My Concubine*, directed by Chen Kaige, another member of the "Fifth Generation" group that revitalized Chinese cinema after the tumultuous Cultural Revolution period.

Gong and Zhang ended their long-term personal relationship while *Shanghai Triad* was in production, and some observers feared this bad "chemistry" might sour the movie. But happily, most critics have applauded her for yet another rich performance, reconfirming her as one of today's most versatile actresses. "She is a very good actress," Zhang enthusiastically agrees. "We have a very successful collaboration, and without her, many of my movies would not be so good."

Accordingly, he seems open to the idea of future teamwork with her. "Any good director likes to work with a good actress," he says. "There's a Chinese saying: As long as there's the right time element and the right people are together, anything is possible."

Cinema and Zhang Yimou

KWOK-KAN TAM/1996

M Y MEETING WITH DIRECTOR Zhang Yimou in Beijing on 25 August 1996 was prefaced by a three-day delay. My thanks must go to Mr. Hu Xiaofeng, the production manager, for he was largely responsible for the arrangement of this meeting. Finally, at Shangri-La Beijing, Director Zhang and I had a fruitful discussion that lasted from 2:00 p.m. to 4:30 p.m.

My appointment with Director Zhang was planned much earlier and finally settled in early August 1996. At that time, I was working on the book *New Chinese Cinema* (co-authored with Wimal Dissanayake, Oxford University Press, 1998), and the interview was planned as part of the book. On the first few days of my arrival in Beijing, I noticed that both of us were burdened by tight schedules, especially Zhang Yimou. He was so busily engaged at that time for the filming of his film, *Keep Cool* (*You hua haohao shuo*) that he simply could not spare a moment. As the whole production team worked with him, he felt bad leaving the team for a personal interview. His attitude that rated films over personal business not only impressed me but also captured my respect.

The interview was conducted in Putonghua and translated into English by myself with the assistance of Ki Wing Chi, who was research assistant at the Chinese University of Hong Kong and is currently reading her Ph.D. in English at University of Edinburgh. Here is the interview.

TAM (KWOK-KAN): *As a renowned photographer, actor, and director, which is your favorite role?*

Printed by permission of the author.

ZHANG (YIMOU): Director.

TAM: *Of all three roles, why do you prefer to be a director?*
ZHANG: Because I think directors are in the best position to express their personalities. We all know how directors can determine the direction of a film so that actors or photographers must conform and confine themselves to a certain boundary. Of course, actors and photographers do possess a certain degree of freedom, but I think only directors can enjoy the sole privilege of self-expression. And their influence towards their films can be unique and ubiquitous. I believe filmmakers all want to manifest their views about the world, about human beings, about life, about feelings. Hence, directors are better positioned to convey their messages to the audience in their films.

TAM: *You are the photographer in* Yellow Earth, *but many people feel that your contributions have surpassed the director's. What would you say to this?*
ZHANG: I don't really think so. Chen Kaige and I were schoolmates at the film school. As we are old friends, we began our film right after we finished school in the spirit of oneness. And that was almost twelve years ago; our relationships were so close that the division of roles was not clear at the time except that he was the director, I was the photographer, and He Qun was the artistic director. And we used to discuss almost everything with each other. As we were fresh graduates, we were energetic, and we entertained high hopes and ambitions to rouse the world. So you can't really say which part of the film belongs to whom. And I myself regard this film as an expression of youth and solidarity. It symbolizes our spirit, our pursuit, and our feelings towards the generation at that time. It is such a corroborated project that blurs the I-You boundary and people can't really say which one is more important than the other is. I feel that *Yellow Earth* marks the spirit of teamwork and solidarity.

TAM: *The way you put it shows your esteem towards your friends. But I have read an article by Chen Kaige saying that many scenes in* Yellow Earth *are your ideas and creations. In that regard, the success of* Yellow Earth *is largely due to your effort.*
ZHANG: Well, I still think the director played the most important part in the making of this film. Though it is Chen Kaige's first film, it was he who

first made the demand to instill our views and critiques towards land, people, and tradition in the film. As a photographer, my role was to fulfill his demand. Of course, as we used to discuss everything together, my concern went beyond graphical conception to technical productions. And we used to work through the construction of script and characters to exchange our views. In the film, many scenes display strong expressiveness to convey powerful feelings. And that is the result of our cooperation with the director because we had lived in Shanbei for quite some time. In order to do all the shooting, we experienced the rugged terrain and the primitive lifestyle of the peasants. Eventually, our long stay in Shanbei left deep impressions on all of us so that we felt the same towards Shanbei, towards the land. And these feelings came out naturally through our cameras. So I think a good photographer is not just responsible for handling visual images or photographic techniques, he should try to understand the essence of the film and convey that aura through the combination of different images. But I still believe this film is a product of solidarity.

T A M : *When we talk about* Yellow Earth, *many critics focus on the opening, contrastive scene that juxtaposes the sky, the land, and the human. But I think the rain dance at the end of the film is even more significant. In these series of shots, the audience can see the masses heading for the same direction while there is one child, alone, taking the reverse path. Are there any multiple implications in your handling of this scene? Are you trying to pinpoint optimism in the midst of pessimism? As we can see, the child is likely to fall onto the ground at any moment, such effort to take a different road can only mean danger. Or maybe the ending of the film is not so optimistic after all.*

Z H A N G : I leave the rights of interpretation to the audience. At that time, we felt such an ending would be better for we could pass on some deep thoughts for the audience to think and feel. We do not have a definite answer. Human beings are such ambiguous animals that definiteness can destroy the message.

T A M : *Though many years have passed, people still remember* Yellow Earth *with its ambiguity. Now* Yellow Earth *has become a classic in the history of contemporary Chinese cinema, but audiences and critics alike are still interested in knowing your feelings at that time when you worked with Chen Kaige. But my concern is different: as a director, what kind of things or events have impressed or influenced you most?*

ZHANG: When I was young, I did not have any intention of becoming a film director. My early years had nothing to do with films at all. Neither my relatives nor my parents were artists, and the film world was so remote and alien to me. My family is from Xi'an, not Beijing. In Beijing, you can get to know a lot of people, but my life was remote to such a world. In this regard, I am very different from Chen Kaige and other people because Chen practically grew up in this field. It was only in the year 1978 when chance had brought me to the Beijing Film School that I began to learn about and know films. In China, the thinking still prevails that the field you major in at college will eventually determine your lifelong profession. Hence, as I look back now, my desire to go to the film school did not come from my love of film, and I had no thoughts of taking up an artistic career. At that time, the Cultural Revolution was just over. Like many other young people, I applied for admission to a tertiary institution because I wanted to change my life. When to go abroad was just an impossible dream, the only way out is to go to school so as to get away from my seven-year job in the factory. So I majored in film and was introduced into this field. My first intention was to stay in Beijing after my graduation, but the lack of networking and connection had failed me. Instead, the state sent me to Guangxi. Once I had chosen this career, I began to like films. And such is the tidings of fate. Like an intruder that enters in the middle of a story, nobody or no work carries an undying influence on me. Of course, there are many brilliant directors and films in China or in foreign countries that I like very much, but none of these masters has struck me deeply. As I have always considered myself an outsider in the film world, I don't cherish such mood or experience. I am not saying that these masters don't deserve respect, it is just that I do not have such background training.

TAM: *Can we put it this way, it is due to your lack of background training that makes you freer to create your own style?*

ZHANG: You may say so. Because I don't understand films, so I must do my own thinking. Before 1978, my knowledge about films was strictly limited to the presentation of the eight-step formula in the revolutionary model plays. Thus I was flabbergasted by my first experience in the film school in 1978 when they showed us a film on police adventure. Action, fights, beauty, car chasing, etc. I was absolutely shocked. And that was in 1978. When you watch my films, you may notice my love of strong contrastive colors. But in fact, all of my early works and photographs were done in black and white. Because I had no money at that time, so not till 1980 could I try my hand on color photography and get my first color photo. Then I began to understand the ways of color. In comparison to Chen Kaige and many other people like him, I was a mature student because they had early access to many films that were open only to "insiders." In a way, my background has enabled me to work with less restriction. And another thing is that my films are in fact constituted by communal or democratic elements. As the mundane experience of my past has become a part of me now, so I used to consider myself as an outsider to the academy. And I am just a regular, normal guy. Hence from *Red Sorghum* to my latest film, you can always find some democratic elements, regardless of their individual styles. And my humble origin can best explain those democratic attributes in my films. But on the contrary, Chen Kaige's films are more philosophical, more critical, and more artistic. On the other hand, I am like my films, more accessible to the mass. My films demonstrate the fact that I am just one of you. But this is not an intentional pursuit.

T A M : *Of all the films you have directed, which one is your favorite?*
Z H A N G : It is difficult to single out one film and regard it as my favorite. And *Red Sorghum, Ju Dou, Raise the Red Lantern, To Live,* and *The Story of Qiu Ju* are definitely in my privileged list, though *Shanghai Triad* is a lesser choice. While the new film I am working on is not yet ready for public review, we can focus on the mentioned five. I would not say that I have zealous appreciation towards them, but I do have true affection for each one because these are all my creations. I think filmmaking is a strenuous task for all directors when it involves complicated issues like financial budgeting, production matters, political concerns, and social problems. Thus I consider it to be very efficient for a director to produce a film within one year or within a year and a half because sometimes it may take two, or even three years to finish off everything. And at the very peak of creativity, most directors can only produce twenty, thirty, or forty films in their entire artistic life span. Given such a difficult job, I can only say that I like fifty percent of my works and the other fifty percent are just so-so.

TAM: *Of the five films you have just mentioned, many critics notice a remarkable thematic shift, that is, from the historical motif at the early phase to the everyday life concern at a later phase. Do you agree with this view, or do you think such change is contingent because you are not bound to any particular motif?*

ZHANG: I don't think I am bound to any motif at all, and neither have I deliberately chosen any set topic to mark my style. But during the emergence of the Fifth Generation films, the interest in historical motifs or peasant issues was undeniable. I think that has to do with the general political environment at the time that eventually influenced the creative mood. Such political environment can be differentiated into two types: the first opportunity came in the early 1980s when China was reforming and opening herself up. And the assimilation of foreign cultures eventually inspired active developments in literature, music, and art. Of all, the three most important developments were nativist literature, reflexive literature, and the literature of the scar. Then all of a sudden, there was a surge of solidarity that compelled everyone to reflect on our cultural tradition, our historical past. As a result, people worked from the primitive, basic principles to rediscover the value of human beings. So that was the social stimulation at the time to prod us to produce works that center on history or peasantry. Such background gave us the creative edge and we were influenced by it. So that's the first general political environment. The second one is the indistinctness of our urban culture. When you look at Beijing, Shanghai, Shenzhen today, it would still be difficult to say that they have established their unique urban style. Most of the time they are merely imitations, modeling upon Western culture, lifestyle, or art. The disorientation after the open-door policy in the 1970s or 1980s has not yet been cleared up. So China is still unable to construct an exclusively Chinese urban culture. Whenever you walk around, all the hotels look alike, all the streets are alike, and the whole city is inundated with imported goods, tobaccos, wine, English, and Western attire. It might be a transitional historical development; however, I think the mass duplication of American popular culture, Hollywood films, popular songs from Taiwan or Hong Kong, or the mass idolization of pop stars by youngsters can strangle the very personality of our urban culture. With the lack of personality, little good stuff can come out. Even though some of them might have succeeded, their scarcity must limit their influence and make them utterly powerless to resist the mainstream cultural conditions. Under such circumstances, whether the directors like it or not, the Fifth Generation films cannot go beyond these two themes. And these two themes have distinguished history and peasantry. But after the 1990s, many people tried to work on similar stories due to the success of some Fifth Generation films. As a result, the abuse of such themes is frequent. Another change in the 1990s is the emergence of an unnamable desire and disturbance in these urban cities. The more these cities change, the more they diversify, and when more and more people aggregate in these cities, more and more things happen. Thus not only Fifth Generation filmmakers, but also all directors take city as the creative locus in the 1990s. Of course, it goes without saying that every director has his own preference, but the general direction all points towards the city. Even though there may be some exceptions. Some directors may insist on producing their own brand of films, but I still think one cannot isolate the individual from the currents of history. So the way I look at things is that, after the 1990s, the urban motif will become the dominant mode and provoke extensive interest and discussion.

TAM : *I would like to ask a question that is related to urban culture. The process of globalization has recently been a hot topic for discussion in the field of social sciences. As globalization means global westernization with the delivery of western cultural patterns, values, social institutions, lifestyles to Asian countries and to the third world, such movement invites various criticisms. On the one hand, this marks a new wave of cultural invasion, but on the other hand, this can affirm the threatening of local culture so as to produce a monologic lifestyle. Just a moment ago, you mentioned the sameness of Chinese city and the similarity of street scenes, does this mirror the process of globalization in Chinese city? In an interview, you have once expressed the desire to lead Chinese films to head for the world but given the effects of globalization that can only heighten threats and oppress local culture, what is your view? If there exist two pathways that can forward Chinese films to the world, one is the patronizing path that courts the favors of foreigners, and the other is the individualizing route to champion your distinctive style, which way would you choose? Can you be more specific with regard to the road that you take with the hope of heading for the world?*

ZHANG : I think globalization is becoming a universal tendency by now. In the recent twenty or thirty years, whichever country you visit, you are bound to experience the feelings of déjà vu. My opinion is that mass media are highly responsible for this because in the past people communicated to each other mostly through radio broadcast, but now we can visualize images on television via satellite. The transmission of images from country to country enables us to witness events worldwide. As an artist devoted to mass media, I think the power of visual effects can never be overrated. With a concrete image, we can dissolve boundaries and allow one to see, think, and feel. So images can be more influential than abstract information or voices because imagination or sound must involve the distance of perception. With the open-door policy of China in the last two decades, everyone is more or less influenced by the mass media for we mostly communicate and learn through images. Under such circumstances, the process of acquisition and imitation through visual media becomes a trendy concern. And gradually, local trends will be assimilated into global trends when images cross national or geographical boundaries. And it is only logical to predict such global assimilation through mass media will go on at a breakneck speed. My view towards globalization is that individuality should always conquer conformity. As a filmmaker is a creator, a creator must have originality, be it fashionable or unfashionable. And to be original is to be unique, to be different. This is very important to me. Though I fully understand the inevitability of superficial resemblance, my love for originality in my own films is fundamental, for I insist on individuality in the midst of similarity. To be frank, an urban story is like the reproduction of an objective reality; I cannot ask my characters to put on the peasants' clothes or act as if they were peasants. If my focus is on objective reality, I must respect its objectivity. Thus in my film, the costume, the houses, the cars must resemble those in the West. This is reality, and I must observe that. But the loss of peculiar images or characters can be compensated by a cultivation of individual perspectives. And that is style. The difference amidst sameness. In order to face the world, to confront China, or to portray individual life, I maneuver my camera so as to capture reality with emphasis on a unique perspective, unique aura. I think this is very important, and at the same time far more difficult than the handling of historical and rustic themes. In the past, the display of Chineseness was easy with the portrayal of peasant livelihood or historical stories because these situations, costumes, and images were unique and exclusive to Chinese society. However, the treatment of urban images can easily reduce the film to a state of banality when urban scenery is everywhere the same. Thus, the urban setting calls for a higher level of originality in scenic treatment. And I must think hard to locate the particularity of each character, of city life. And that goes beyond mere packaging or scenic arrangement. When these exclusively Chinese stories have inspired me in the past, the globalizing tendency poses a tougher challenge to directors and creators. They have to articulate their individual personality and foreground distinctness in indistinctness.

TAM: *In that way, when you are dealing with urban themes, do you have to highlight the transcodified and go beyond the denotative level to probe the connotative level of images?*

ZHANG: When I say urban images have lost their novelty, the cultural or social significance of urban imagery must become more important and subtle. With the depletion of intrinsic meaning, urban symbols have become banal but universal. Even foreigners can identify at first sight whether the character is rich or poor, educated or rustic. When there were fewer things left on the surface, we should try for a deeper understanding of scenes and imagery. And we can no longer treat characters as symbols as in *Yellow Earth*. Time has changed and time has eliminated the unique representation of characters. And scenes must become more allegorical, symbolic nowadays. But here involves a paradox for me when modern films demand a more intellectual, philosophical treatment while I must employ democratic elements to express such intellectual symbols or allegory. I handle my films in this way: when we look back to the first appearance of films a hundred years ago, films were a combination of attics and mass entertainment. In that sense, films are very different from painting, poetry, or music which are abstract and can be refined to enjoy a high degree of purity. For films, their origin was closely linked to collective entertainment and attics; gradually, commercial elements, production, and technology began to complicate things. So films are such chaotic potpourris that they contain all kinds of elements. And we can only bring in the allegorical, symbolic aspects through these elements. If we have to reduce films into abstraction as in painting, poetry, or music, few people will be able to appreciate them. If people can't appreciate, they will boycott them. Given the hybrid nature of films, they must belong to the people and not to the elite. So I think here lies our main contradiction in modern filmmaking: the universal loss of novelty in scenes must call for the search of deeper meanings; and yet deep meanings must work through the use of democratic but stale images. And this is our contradiction—we must bury deep the messages as well as to transmit them. This is the kind of difficulty and problems we have to face in the future. Let's take artistic films, we all want them to revoke our feelings and not just focus on the superficial images. And that has exactly touched upon the problem of hiding and revealing. That is a difficult task, and a task many directors have to face.

TAM: *I think the success of your films lies exactly in your balance of hiding and revealing, so the audience can think and feel at the same time.*
ZHANG: That is what I have intended to do. I want my audience to think when they watch my films. But as a director, I can realize my limitations because I can't change the world with my personal effort. I have to understand the reception of the audience. And I will keep on doing this. After all, what is a film? What is the boundary of audience reception? These questions always occupy my mind, and they have become my principles and habits at work.

TAM: *I would like you to talk about* The Story of Qiu Ju. *Some critics think it is a realist film. They think it is very dramatic. However, I think it is a story about perseverance, to uphold an ideal, but such perseverance can only lead to an ambivalent feeling at the end. So this helps bring out the ambiguity of the film and mingles pessimism with optimism. What is your view?*
ZHANG: I only want to enrich its ambiguities. *The Story of Qiu Ju* is a very strange film, and it is so far my most widely accepted film. Chinese people love it, foreigners loved it, and intellectuals like it and the government likes it too. Many people say, "Zhang Yimou, this is your only film that everyone approves." What I would like to present in that particular film is "perspectivism." Just as the saying goes, what you get is what you see. People can only get what they want to find and what they understand. So everybody says this film is nicely done. Such consensual response is very rare. Even though I intend to produce something everybody likes, the result may not be so. When I worked on *The Story of Qiu Ju*, I had no calculation on its effects. Making a film is a process based on the intense feelings on the part of the director that it is impossible to predict the audience's response. And I have been surprised by the favorable comments I have received so far. In *The Story of Qiu Ju*, the theme, plot, and the story work with each other so well to produce multiple meanings. And the ambivalence and absurdity of life are products of contingent inspiration. I have no intention to say that this film or my creations are clever, but I just followed my instinct to make this film. The rights of interpretation belong not to me but to everybody. I also believe

that various interpretations can be authentic because they can find different traces in the film. This is really special. Not many films can do this. And this is really beyond my design. My original intention was to work on another film because I felt *The Story of Qiu Ju* was basically infeasible. I bought the novel in a street by accident, and after I had read it, I wanted to do a film based on this story. Many methods had been tried, but everything turned out to be unsatisfactory. In the end, I changed the theme and sneaked into the street to shoot the film. At that time, there was such creative impulse that drove me to work on *The Story of Qiu Ju*. Eventually, the voyeuristic angle began to emerge in this story. After the story had begun, it was difficult to say what moved the story on. One should feel content with what one gets. So the development of the story followed the development of the characters, and I simply left the script behind. The only thing I wanted to do at that time was to energize the story, to make it live. My duty was to fulfil this role. When a film is enlivened, even the author cannot hold it back. The author must go along with it to let the film finish itself. If it happens that the film is good, it is just an accident. Of course I wish my other works could be that good, but that is something beyond my control. If I want to produce something transcultural or universal, I can't do it just by following the rules. To be frank, all of my films are products of my gut feelings. If I am touched, I can do it; if I am not touched, I just can't shoot anything. Even though I try hard, I will only step into the wrong areas. I love to create. Since to be creative does not have any fixed rule, I can't foresee the outcome of my labor before it is done.

TAM: *What is the impact of the Cultural Revolution on you?*
ZHANG: The Cultural Revolution was a part of our history. It was an unforgettable experience not only to me, but also to all people of my generation. I grew up during the Cultural Revolution. And I was sixteen at the time with a desire to know everything. Such experience marked deeply on me and on my generation. I didn't deliberately call upon this memory, but it is so deeply rooted in me that it has become a starting point for comparison and contrast in our life. It leads one to reflect on life and on society, to question the established values and meanings. The Cultural Revolution does not have a particular aspect that produces a concrete impact on me. Instead, it is everywhere in my nerve.

TAM: *Some critics think you try to appeal to the foreign audience in your films. What do you say?*

ZHANG: It is nonsense. Such criticisms have existed for a long long time and is becoming stale. I can only say flattery or compliments are not part of my concern because it is technically impossible. Anywhere outside China is already a foreign country, and with so many foreign countries, which country should I appeal to? For me, I don't understand any foreign language, and I have no idea about Westerners' preferences, conventions, and film watching habits. All my visits to foreign film festivals were short, and most of the time I saw only journalists or friends in party receptions. My understanding of Western culture is very superficial and subjective. I don't have the ability to court their favor because if I really want to do so, I must first know them well. Say, if foreigners like "sweet" things, how sweet is their idea of "sweetness"? I am unable to judge at all. Thus it could be difficult for me to court their favor and almost impossible. But such opinion is very popular in China. Regardless of their class background, workers, peasants, intellectuals, and university professors generally have opinions of this kind towards the Fifth Generation films. I think it only mirrors the negative psychology in Chinese personality. Though we have turned away from the "closed-door" policy of self-containment, people in China still harbor all kinds of narrow-mindedness. Maybe there would be no such problem in twenty or thirty years' time, but in the next five or ten years, criticisms of this sort will keep coming up. This can't be helped because one side cannot convince the other. I can't just silence everybody by making a manifesto because many people have already formed their opinions. And that cannot be changed. I can only respect my own feelings, and make films in my own way. I strongly insist that my target audience is Chinese and my films are for China. That is the only thing I can do because my understanding of life, culture, and society is limited to that of the Chinese. Of course I want to do a film for the whole world, but I don't really know much about the world. As a director, I would feel happier if my films can get worldwide appreciation.

TAM: *Of all your films I have seen, though the subjects keep changing, your personal style is very strong and consistent. What do you have to say about the international acclaim you have received for so far?*

ZHANG: First of all, I am delighted. All directors want to reach a large pool of audience. After all, films are for people to see. I am glad that many people know my films or know Chinese films because of me. This success, whether you look at it from a personal angle or from a national angle, is still a wonderful thing. But before that, I have no idea to guess whether they would be popular or not. Since I don't know the West, I can only begin with what I feel. As I myself am an audience, I can look at my film from the audience's perspective to watch my life and my world. So I must be moved before I perceive the significance of any subjects for my films. Thus, my audience and I are not enemies because I am an audience, and I watch other people's films, too. I believe, when I am touched, others would feel the same. Of course, I am not saying that I should force my feelings upon the audience. When I cry, others may not cry at all. Such imposition is doomed to become a failure.

TAM: *Your films are mostly about women. Do you have any special reason for taking women as one of your major concerns?*

ZHANG: I don't think there is any special reason in that. Gong Li and I have worked together for a long, long time. She is a good actress and I admire her a lot. So I like to have her in my films. But at the moment, China is still very different from the West because we don't have any stardom in the film industry. In the West, or in Hong Kong and Taiwan, their major concern is about which film star they can get, then they write a script, design the costume, and set a story particularly for that star. Up to now, we have few or even no production which works that way. We always find a story first and select some suitable themes from various topics, and then we look for suitable actors. And I haven't gone out of my way to find scripts for Gong Li. Personally, I am very interested in women's stories. My films love to construct worlds with fragmentary experiences, and in these fragmentary experiences, there are usually a lot of latent obstacles. I think the meaning of life shines through when characters must survive in the face of obstacles. In the five thousand years' history of China, women's life is definitely the most difficult and unfortunate in spiritual or material terms. When the crisis of characters opens up the meaning of life, that is the essence of art. Fortunate people can seldom reflect the meaning of life, and they can't rouse my interest.

TAM: *Have any contemporary film directors affected or stimulated you strongly after you have watched their films?*

ZHANG: Many directors' films touch me and make me admire them very much. But none of them has any strong influence on me.

TAM: *What is your view on the Sixth Generation films?*
ZHANG: I have not seen many Sixth Generation films because most of them are "underground films" and are not shown openly. First of all, I think China needs the Sixth Generation films, and after the Sixth, there should be the Seventh Generation so that the film industry can move on. But the Sixth Generation film is still a vague term that articulates a wish rather than a reality. It is a wish to go beyond the Fifth Generation and break new grounds. It has yet to establish its own system and its own characteristics. If the Sixth Generation filmmakers want to make history, they need to work harder to put things into a system. They need to define what is the Sixth Generation instead of generalizing vaguely that they are "not the Fifth Generation." Such a marker doesn't clarify anything at all. The Sixth Generation hasn't come into shape because it has made no artistic breakthrough. And that absence of breakthrough has to do with the absence of masters. If they can come up with a few masters, they can lay the foundation of the Sixth Generation and build their own systematic style. I agree with their slogan; that is, "to beat me and Chen Kaige." But I also believe the most important thing is to surpass us and establish a new system and style. But this may take ten years to make it happen. As the Fifth Generation films are still developing without any symptom of decay, to surpass the evolving Fifth Generation requires double hard work. And much of it also depends on historical contingency and artistic achievement.

TAM: *In many of your films, stories are adaptations of literary works. But if we look at it in another way, these works can rouse stronger international repercussions after your adaptations. Or if we put it differently, we have few Chinese writers who are awarded international literary prizes, while many Chinese films have received wide international acclaim and awards. What do you think about this? Do you think Chinese films have attained higher achievements than literature?*
ZHANG: Though my films do not come a hundred percent from literary works, most of them are. I think literature is the origin of my creativity, and the source of future cinematic creations. Thus, I believe Chinese literature should be recognized in the international scene. But as for winning the Nobel Prize, I don't think it is a good yardstick to measure the success of our

literature. Winning a prize is just a propagandistic thing. But we all tend to question in a vague way as to why Chinese films have received international attention, but our literary world has failed to get its share. I believe it is because films do have their artistic advantages in terms of media and forms of expression. Films are blessed in the habit of extensive showing and popular display. I am not saying it is superior to literature. It is just that literary works require translators, publishers, and salespersons in order to reach foreign readers. In that case, the number of foreign readers must be highly limited. With an inadequate promotion and circulation network, literary works usually fail to draw gossip and attract people's attention. So the popularity of Chinese films and the relative obscurity of Chinese literature with regard to reception and circulation are in a way due to their difference in artistic forms. It is not a matter of inferiority that draws such difference. Without good literary works, it could be difficult to produce good films. Films are not constitutive of actions only. Motion without thoughts can only be dead actions. In my films, those images that have touched people deeply are mostly originated from literature. And such literary experience has inspired me. So I believe the relative lack of attention towards our literature is due to its artistic limitations. Regarding form, no art except films have ever received such worldwide reception. Music, painting, poetry have failed to become the object of extensive display. And the popularity of literary works must be confined by the limits of linguistic and cultural understanding. Of course, there are even more complicated considerations with regard to awards. We have many film festivals in a year, and the chances to be selected for film exhibitions are high. But literary awards do not come from exhibition but from a series of procedures like recommendation and evaluation. And many writers do not even have access to such games. Thus it would be far more difficult to win the Nobel Prize than to win an award in film festivals. In terms of historical development, other forms of media have temporarily replaced the function of literature. In the 1990s, the attitude of Chinese towards literature is polarized into either love or indifference. The book lovers keep reading books, and the non-literary type just eschews them. But on the other hand, most people are fond of visual representations. I think it is due to the laziness of the mind. This is a universal phenomenon. This is the tragedy of our time.

TAM: *When you did* Red Sorghum, *you asked the author Mo Yan for advice. And his reply was that he had total confidence in you. So, how do you interpret a literary work and translate it into film language?*

ZHANG: It is difficult to say. Different works call for concrete interpretations. In general, I believe in my feelings. If I am moved, I can translate that into visual terms. But as literary works are rich and multiple in meanings, a total translation into film language could be difficult. My way of appropriation appeals to essence and forgoes the form. Or I just select a part and forget the whole. I tend to magnify one aspect and focus on the gist of it. If you have to add too many things to a film, it becomes a book. But films call for simplicity, sensibility, and directness. Only with these things can we produce the strongest impact. Like the adaptation of *Red Sorghum*, I did not aim at the total representation of the original work. Instead, I elaborated on the theme of "the power of life," on the question of "humanity" and transformed them into pictorial images. Such decision is made for the sake of concentration and refinement. And it can avoid the pitfall of telling a full story but showing a limp plot. One of the advantages for films is to attain strong impact with strong images. But such impact requires a high degree of concentration and must avoid divergence from the main theme. That is also the weakness of filmic expression. Unlike films, novels always call for the development of multiple plots, multiple consciousness in order to amplify their imaginary space. And prose is similar to films in terms of its precise expression to produce strong impact. When I try to adapt literary works into films, I single out some "points" and work on them for further elaboration. I can't just leave the whole story unchanged onto the silver screen; and neither can I translate those literary works into films without my own interpretation.

TAM: *Thank you very much for the interview. And I hope we can see more of your upcoming films in the near future.*

Discussing *Keep Cool*: The Camera Lens Presents the Irrationality of Chinese Society

JIAO XIONGPING/1998

I've just seen Keep Cool—*its great! Thank you for arranging for me to view it. Could you talk about why this film was invited to Cannes yet was unable to go?*
That was ridiculous. The government didn't publicly announce their position on Cannes. A month passed after we'd submitted our report, and the government didn't want to let us go, so they used Zhang Yuan's *East Palace, West Palace* as an excuse.

In the opinion of the government—including the Vice-minister of Culture Zhao Shi and Film Bureau Chief Wang Gengnian-this film was to go to Hawaii to reduce its influence; it was to be handled "low-key." We could distribute the film domestically, but the movie theaters were all dominated by films that sang to the government's tune. So they didn't have time to show my film—the government had decided on "low-key" handling and didn't feel that this film should be allowed to be influential.

Since the Changsha Conference, the watchful attitude of government seems to have become stricter, hasn't it?
There's nothing we can do about it. We try our best to make a film whenever there's an opportunity to make one, but it's getting more and more difficult to make films. The situation doesn't look very good. The government censors have become stricter and the new leaders cleverer than before.

I didn't argue and allowed them to cut several places or drop this or that

From *Turbulent Meetings: Dialogues with Contemporary Chinese Film* (Yuanliu Publishing: Taiwan). Translated by Stephanie Deboer.

sentence. They always notified us through written documents and never spoke with us. We'd just revise our written reports, they wouldn't be satisfied, and so we'd revise again. We went back and forth like this three or four times over two months from beginning to end. The government didn't leave any room for discussion, so we went through a lot of fruitless effort.

We all felt that we were being stifled in our undertakings—that the creative atmosphere around us was oppressive, full of more frustrations than before, narrower than before, and that the censors were even stricter than before. It's the period of Deng Xiaoping versus the times of Jiang Zemin. It was also an aftereffect of June Fourth.

This, of course, has influenced our frame of mind—no one is happy in terms of creativity. All this flourishing of worldly desire and monetary pleasure in society, yet film isn't prospering.

This is very similar to the content of your Keep Cool.
Yes. This is an urban farce. Events are all magnified and take on an exaggerated style to depict reality.

According to the opening film credits, your film is adapted from Shu Ping's original work, Evening News.
I revised this story so many times over the course of a year. Originally, it was a story about three men and three women, but I later got rid of some of the story lines. I've now only preserved from the original story the conversation in the bar. Where he originally cut someone's hand, he was cut by someone else, and character relationships and roles were all changed. The original book was about a boiler worker and a fellow work unit member, but now it's about someone's computer being smashed to bits against a telephone pole.

I like the sense of absurdity in Shu Ping's fiction, his urban people's fatalistic attitudes—small things aren't a big deal—and their completely illogical ways of dealing with things.

We wrote the script in a year and had two large-scale discussions. Everyone including the directors of photography, music, and art, the assistant director, and the actors all attended and discussed. We also used a beta cam to test shoot, first cutting a sample print to make sure we were consistent in the feeling of the film.

Your aesthetics have changed immensely this time, with impromptu performances and a greatly shaking camera lens. Could you explain your aesthetic design?

This time my filming methods have really gone in the opposite direction from the past. I completely followed my feelings and the camerawork was rather impromptu. The cameras followed the performers, and the actors also performed extemporaneously. We could have shot eight cuts, and each one would have been different.

I'll admit that there's a definite sense of risk-taking and challenge this time; everyone thinks that I haven't been able to capture a sense of balance. An average of fifteen cuts was shot for every scene, and the editing was fun, with so many options that it was chaotic. The performers incessantly rattled on, talking in circles—they talked sheer nonsense, speaking spontaneously over and over again, repeating themselves.

Jiang Wen and Li Baotian spoke very fast the first time they attempted to do this. We used a stopwatch to keep time, wanting them to increase their speed but not think about it in order to destroy their linguistic habits.

As a result, actually, a distinctive temperament of Chinese people emerged, particularly in terms of relationships among mainland Chinese; they don't go along with or trust the law, and societal order is often solved through extreme methods. Let me give you an example. It's just like the issue of housing distribution. Staff and workers might go and sleep in their factory director's doorway to voice their demands until the director is so tired of it that he or she gives them a unit.

Actually, the shaking of the camera lens this time was also used to present this kind of irrationality. Big contemporary Chinese cities of the nineties generally move restlessly, brimming with desire. Everyone is in an impulsive, restless state, and there's no sense of reason in their outlook—they aren't objective. You don't know how any matter will develop and just have to see how things go.

Chinese society and Western society are different. The West is full of fin-de-siècle, decadent feelings that reflect on the oppression of the material world. But the mainland is the opposite—with money, material goods, de-sires—and filled with competition and opportunity. It's the desire of all humanity to want to live even better, to want to get rich. Of course, some foreign admirers have borrowed from the West things like the lonely oppression of the world, but generally speaking, it's still money worship and opportunism. Mao Zedong's times thought that money was disgraceful, but now both material goods and money have been introduced into society. This film attempts to capture Chinese people's particular attitudes and ways of looking at problems. It's realistic, but it also utilized an exaggerated style to magnify things. Mainland people are exactly like this—they'll chat for days about the size of a sesame seed. Everyone will stand by their opinion and make it into a big deal by unreasonably fighting about it endlessly.

I also feel that it's very realistic. I would call it the city version of The Story of Qiu Ju—*a few people are caught in something for which they feel they must find a solution and then get tangled up in complications of feeling, reason, and law.*
We say that no two things are compatible, but Jiang Wen and Li Baotian are of the same mold—it's like a modern fable. In the last five minutes of the film, the two exchange places. Jiang Wen repeats what Li Baotian had done to him. He gives himself a shake and changes identity—the times change.

Would you say that the camera lens moves this much in order to capture the rest-lessness of modern people?
Yes. Modern people are impulsive and simply have no sense of reason or complicated inner feelings. It seems that what audiences couldn't tolerate in *Qiu Ju* was the complicated inner nature of the characters. They had contra-dictions of spirit and body, they were in a dilemma, they said one thing and meant another, and they became more complicated inside as they came to understand reason and morality. Therefore, my camera had to be stable, and had to look into the inner being of the characters as well as the flash of their eyes to observe their inner worlds. The camera of *Keep Cool*, on the other hand, was to reflect the mentality of contemporary people. Because of this, the camera utilized a symbolic method—it's the epitome of the contempo-rary person, moving restlessly and often reversing roles. I'm in you and you're in me. What's right could be wrong, and what's wrong could be right. There was really no way for the camera to have objective distance. Instead, it had impromptu freedom.

Although you emphasized spontaneity, I feel that within all of this there's still a strong sense of design, exact and comparatively reserved.
I'll admit to this—it goes without saying that art is self-conscious. Directors are all alike, and no one is an exception here. Over the course of their filming careers, directors should increasingly have a goal—not necessarily of material gain, but the goal should become increasingly complicated and clear to you. So generally speaking, a director's earlier works are rather flexible, but all this

disappears in their middle or late periods. This is a regular kind of pattern—people can't run counter to nature. When reason starts to come into play, it's no longer possible to rely on the feelings or preserve the child-like state of your early period. It seems as if we're saying that once you've lost your virginity, you'll never get it back!

I think that while more mature directors shouldn't go for the empty spirit of primitivism, they should naturally display their inner feelings. Nonetheless, directors have to face all kinds of decisions and choices every day; it's impossible not to be self-aware. Also, the availability of external information is making things increasingly complex, so it's inevitable that directors place things under more and more careful consideration.

Some people say that I copied Wang Kar-wai in becoming formalistic. Actually, with so few methods available to film, there's no incorrect way of doing things, because there are only these few devices. No one can avoid being told that this form has been already used by someone else. Because of this, I won't treat anything as taboo as long as it suits the theme.

Let me put it this way. A film is just a film. To speak bluntly, you may have lots of ability and ambition like hell, but you'll only be the topic of conversation for three months—perhaps a few feverish fans may talk of you a bit longer—and I'd say that only around ten thousand people in the whole world will talk about you like this. For everyone else, it's over in three days. So it's enough to try your best to make a film and disregard how others talk about you. In the past, I always took things too hard—it was tough. I asked myself what would I do if Cannes happened to condemn me. Nowadays, I'm never concerned about honor or disgrace. I can't do anything about what I can't do, so I don't take it too much to heart. I just do what I can.

The style of your recent films—from The Story of Qiu Ju *up to* To Live, Shanghai Triad, *and* Keep Cool—*has changed greatly. Why?*
I'm extremely pleased about this—I don't want to be repeating myself. Regardless of whether they're successful or not, I'll always have something to look forward to. And if I can maintain an attitude of change, I'll always be able to change greatly. You almost can't see my earlier works in *Keep Cool*, but in changing this much, I've prolonged my resiliency. It would serve me right to lose after exercising myself in this way.

Actually, I'd like to make a film every year, but I'm not able to do this right now. It isn't a question of funding or workforce, but rather of subject matter—you can't make bricks without straw. With this kind of lack of prosperity, I can only fill up the vacancies by directing an opera, not attending to my usual duties, and judging film exhibitions—from the Locamo, to the San Sebastian festivals—because there's no work for me to do.

Actually, I love film. Other arts don't attract me. But, it's extremely difficult with this lack of creative freedom. I actually envy Hong Kong and Taiwanese directors.

You seem to have changed your way of dealing with performers this time.
When I directed Gong Li in the past, I did everything on her behalf due to my own personal feelings—I felt responsible for her and never wanted to let her down. My roles were all shaped with her individual personality in mind—I didn't have her dig deeply but let her play herself. When she asked me what to do about her lines, I had her say them as herself.

Looking at it from this perspective, aspects of Jiang Wen and Li Baotian are also in their characters this time. Jiang Wen is very arrogant—he looks down on everyone—and Li Baotian is very principled. Also, as I said earlier, I asked the two of them to speak very fast, fight endlessly, and talk in circles.

I've known you for many years, and this is the first time I've felt that you've become much more relaxed and open.
I don't let things bother me so much any more. I've reconciled myself to criticism and praise of my works and my personal life, even reconciled myself to the affair with Gong Li. Whenever there was a problem or a mishap in the past, I wouldn't be able to sleep. During *Raise the Red Lantern*, I often thought that I wasn't filming it very well, and then I'd get no sleep as I spent hours thinking about it.

As a matter of fact, as far as energy and judgement are concerned, I'm now in my prime, but unfortunately the times are uncertain and closed. I can only try to maintain my abilities and creative flexibility as much as possible within this limited space and just wait and see whether my style will change or not. I think that *Keep Cool* is a personal film. I rather admire my own bit of courage—its style is quite bold. My earlier filming of *One and Eight* and *Yellow Earth* both emphasized an unmoving frame, but this time I cut until I was dizzy.

I'm really proud of these kinds of "alternative films." I don't like popular

films, because they don't make an impact on me—I don't admire or appreciate them. I also strive to make alternative films.

Let's talk about your directing an opera!
Opera is a highly refined and excellent art form. The complex perfection of
its chorus and ensembles, as well its audience's custom of wearing formal
attire, was all a whole new world for me—it could mold your taste, sentiment, and temperament. As I directed it, I was so moved several times that I
trembled. The first time was during rehearsal, when the male and female
soloists began with that grand sound and elegance—even though I didn't
understand, I was still moved. It seemed that I would shed tears, the music
was so full of emotion.

The second time I trembled was when the chorus entered—oh, their
voices were brilliant. And the third time was when the music director, Zubin
Mehta, came onto the stage. Once he began rehearsing, I simply couldn't
bring myself to stop him. I sat there and listened, with him thinking it
strange that I didn't stop him—he kept looking at me.

Zubin and I later came to a tacit agreement. He would wink at me at every
good point in the music.

So how did you direct the opera?
Like a film—I only asked that it not be boring. Although I didn't understand,
I did hope that no one would doze off over the three hours and added various
things that were in keeping with the refinement of the opera, that carried
poetic flavor and charm and that integrated Eastern artistic concepts. At the
same time, I designed a bit of a visual climax every five to ten minutes. During the opening performance, I sat there feeling anxious, noting with my
assistants that this light was late, that thing was placed in the wrong spot, or
this performer walked too fast. There were twenty-six mistakes in all, which
constantly distressed me. I didn't expect that after the performance the ap-
plause would be like thunder, that it would be this successful.

I went there with the aim of doing everything in the service of the singing—whenever someone suggested something I simply changed it. We began
rehearsing my second day in Milan and rehearsed for twenty-one or twenty-
two days altogether. I don't understand music, but in the end we finished
rehearsing in less than a month. The chorus told me that of all their direc-

tors, I'd had them move the most and that the lighting had been more sensitive and complicated than other operas, emphasizing artistic conception.

In addition, I brought with me concepts of Chinese opera. In all of China's
twenty provinces and municipalities, there isn't one opera that isn't brightly
colored. Whenever someone wears something colorful, we'll always say, "So
you've come wearing opera costume!" So I brought with me the gorgeous,
colorful costumes of Shaanxi and Beijing opera and filled the stage with
color—even the Italians said that they needed to wear dark glasses to watch
it. I didn't care and added more brightness, added more lighting, and ignored
European tastes. I went against the tide, making it all absolutely brilliant.

These foreigners had a blind confidence in me, saying that because Toura-
ndot was a Chinese subject matter, then I was the authority—I had my reasons for using the lighting like this. As a result, everyone praised it.

Were the audience and critical reactions all good?
They said that it was the best version of Puccini's opera in thirty years—that
I took an incomplete opera and presented its full features for the first time.
Later came ten or so critics. Even the fastidious ones all said it was good and
only pointed out some shortcomings of Zubin and the chorus.

Zubin and I became friends. I really admire him—he has patience, he isn't
anxious, and he takes his time to refine everything. I really hated to go when
I left, but the opera will come to perform in Beijing this year.

I brought the sense of sight, the color, costume, and mise en scène of
Chinese opera to *Turandot*. East and West really combined harmoniously. At
the end, I set up eight opera stages, on which I placed such operas as *Farewell
My Concubine, Dragon Phoenix, Women Generals of the Yang Family,* and *Journey
to the West.* Above, the foreigners sang and below them Mu Guiying flew
across the stage with banners displayed on her back—it was a magnificent
sight.

Not One Less

CYNTHIA WU / 1998

IN MAY 1998, TEN days after Zhang Yimou's new movie started rolling, a Santana [type of Volkswagon sold in China) took me and my curiosity to Zhang Jiakou, a small city about four hours' drive from Beijing to interview this famous director. The movie they are shooting is called *Not One Less*, and I myself do not want to miss this opportunity.

Getting an interviewing with Zhang Yimou is difficult. Even in my hometown Beijing, I felt he was harder to reach than he was in Montreal last winter. Zhang Yimou is constantly hounded by the paparazzi, so it is not surprising that reporters must contact his producer first, Hu Xiaofeng, and then be put on a long waiting list along with other interview seekers from across the world. And finally wait for a vacancy in the crew's van, which only runs once a week to the filming location, Zhang Jiakou—which literally means: the village of Zhang's family—a remote city about four hours drive north of Beijing. As well as interviewing Zhang, I had the chance to talk to Cao Jiuping, his long-time art director, and Zhang Yimou's cinematographer and one-time classmate Hou Yong.

At the point of arrival, I noticed that some of his crewmembers were wearing the T-shirt with the words "Zhang Yimou's crew" and stamped with a list of his works from *Red Sorghum* to *Yigedoubunengshao* (*Not One Less*) to the Italian opera *Turandot* [directed by Yimou], and even his then forthcoming film "My Father and My Mother [*The Road Home*]."

It was arranged for me to settle down with them in one of the best hotels

---

Printed by permission of the author.

in Zhang Jiakou. Just after I unpacked my suitcase, a little girl hopped in front of me, and asked: "Are you here with us, sister?" She looked at me curiously and naively. Producer Hu Xiaofeng introduces her: "This is Wei Minzhi, the main actress." I later learn that Wei, an ordinary country school-girl, was discovered by the director out of thousands of local rivals. Apart from her, the ten other starring children are all first-time actors chosen from over 10,000 participants. I perceive the thirteen-year-old Wei to be still a child mentally and physically.

"We want her to look authentic and simple. The girl's simple disposition fits the character in the movie." The producer explained further, "During the filming, we tried our best to keep her the way she is. She is not allowed to watch TV because we believe television would make her know too much of the outside world. And the worst scenario would be that some not-so-healthy information might make her mature quickly. We do not want this to happen. So, we hired a schoolteacher to accompany her and advance her studies. In the movie, she is a teacher for the whole school, and she has to manage students who are older than she."

During the lunch hour, Zhang Yimou showed up in the canteen, in red T-shirt and black jeans. Zhang had nothing special for his meal: minced meat, sliced potatoes, steamed bun, and egg soup. It is my first time encoun-tering the legendary Zhang Yimou in such ordinary circumstances. I was sur-prised to see how he kept such a simple lifestyle, while his extraordinary productions have swept through so many international festivals: *Red Sor-ghum*, *The Story of Qiu Ju*, *To Live*, and many other masterpieces of Chinese cinema. And Zhang never complained about the harsh conditions of the locations.

Not One Less deals with the dropout problem in China's rural areas. The story focuses on the thirteen-year-old substitute teacher, Wei Minzhi, and her tremendous efforts to keep her pupils in school to receive an education. Her efforts include searching for a student who has gone missing in a city so she can keep the film's titular promise to her students: "No One Less."

On the first night the scene took place at an old-fashioned TV station about forty minutes drive from our hotel. In the story Wei Minzhi comes here to seek help after discovering that her student Zhang Huike is missing. Two local anchorwomen of the station broadcast her announcement. Zhang Yimou, directing the filming from the monitor outside of the room looks serious and full of concentration. At times he utters *"Kaishi"* (action) or *"ting"* (stop), his voice low but firm and powerful. During the break, I asked him a question: why did the topic of children seize his heart this time? He replies, "It is about how a kid succeeded in doing something all by herself. It is a touching story. This movie is one of the most challenging projects I have ever taken. But it is the most rewarding one for sure." His assistant adds that what brings more strength to the production is that this story describes the countryside children's extraordinary endeavor in pursuing knowledge. As a result the movie will raise the issue of education for kids in impoverished regions for the whole society. (As a side note, at the end of the filming the crew donated a brand-new school to the village—Shuiquan Elementary School.)

From *Red Sorghum*'s ballad approach to his realistic pinnacle *The Story of Qiu Ju*, critics say that Zhang Yimou changed the way the world visualizes China and helped alter the course of Chinese cinema. In his earlier movies Zhang Yimou experimented with trying out different styles. *Red Sorghum* is known for a folk-ballad approach; while *The Story of Qiu Ju* stands out as the first "social-realist film of its kind in the Chinese cinema." The crew for this new film, like *The Story of Qiu Ju*, is using a realistic documentary style. But, as Zhang explains, in many ways it is also very different. It is the first of Zhang's movies to adopt an entire cast of non-professional performers.

I talked with Zhang Yimou during a break in filming.

1. On the style of his new movie

c w : *How did you define the realistic style of this movie? How did you come to use such inexperienced young actors and actresses?*

z y : The "realistic style" of the movie was decided when we discussed the script. The crew was trying to find out which style was the best. We put our ideas together and reached an agreement to use this "animated documentary" approach to present the story. However, it is a fictional feature film, not a documentary. Even documentaries, I think, have a certain percentage of subjective content. When an incident happens, unless you were there on the spot and documented the whole process with your camera, I would not say the movie would be a pure documentary with an objective approach. It is like an interview. We are here to talk about the past. The information is on the feedback of an incident in the past. We are presenting our own subjective point of view.

Using non-professional actors is another distinctive feature of this film. I decided on this because I felt that, professional or not, the actors are doing something that never happened in their lives. The drama was made up; it only happens in the story. Even though I used actors sharing similar life experiences with the characters, they are not doing the action exactly the same as they did in their own past. What they can do is to imitate or recast certain plots that are similar to the past. The schoolteachers, headmasters, and boss of a television station, even the doorman, are people who play those roles in life. Some of them have been doing the same job for twenty years.

c w : *How did you manage the balance of making a fiction film in a realistic documentary style?*
z y : Fiction film is really different from documentary in this aspect. It is less objective because the director expresses a subjective point of view with the movie. I would like the movie to look like a documentary, look real. "Real" refers to a realistic style. While making a fiction film, we are using the documentary style to reflect the reality. What is a fiction film? I think it is a process of emulating, reflecting what has happened in reality.

Using "realistic style" does not mean that we have to change and make a documentary film. It remains fiction. When I make movies, it is subjective—my own interpretation of the novel, my way of organizing the movie scenes. The director's reflection is not objective because we are expressing our own point of view and from the angle of what interests us.

c w : *I noticed that you have always paid special attention to the spectacular effects of the images, such as in* Red Sorghum . *As a director, previously a cinematographer, how did you manipulate the narration of the visual aspects of this film?*
z y : It is true that I was a cinematographer, so for me, the narration of the spectacular is powerful and important. I always pay special attention to the expression of the images. It has always been my style. In this new movie, we are trying to transmit a realistic message to the audience through the visuals. Similar to the way of filming in *The Story of Qiu Ju* (1992), we placed our camera in a hidden place to handle the scenes. The camera responds to the natural scenes, people come in and out, not knowing that they are being "observed" by the eyes of the camera. On the other hand, I always pay attention to the quality of the image. Aesthetically, I found what comes out with this method is remarkably beautiful. It is beautiful even though it is

imperfect. It is something we could never copy or create in reality. The most important thing is that to achieve the effect of an organized frame, we are likely to adjust the elements within; it just becomes a habit. We could never reach such a high state of naturalness, being so real and true. It adds credit to our movie. When the film was nearly finished, the crewmembers and I all felt that this would be a good film, and the audience will love it. I am quite sure about this.

2. About popular culture and the West

C W : *How do you interpret pop culture in mass media?*

Z Y : I think being popular is a tool instead of a purpose. One has to use a tool to express what he wants to express. Sometimes movies from the West are using this as a purpose for a high market value. Their movies are made to be trendy so that they could attract a great number of people. And in turn, they will make money that way. This is a universal feature in the industry. But for me I do not feel that it is enough if you just want to make something so that it will be popular. I have to express what I want to say. I probably would refuse to make such a film. To cast a movie, I have to find myself, to express what I want. For me, being popular is a process to make more and more people accept your ideas. For the movies I make, I try my best to make them popular, to make the audience accept it naturally. This is important. But I do not mean the other extreme, to only express what you want to say and neglect the public. This could end up as something just cherished by the artist. I think we are part of the mass, not higher than other people. I do not think possessing the quality of being popular is something to lose face over. It is a style. It would work for the movies if and only if I am able to express what I want to say and use popularity as a tool.

C W : *Your movies have won a lot of international awards. Is this just a coincidence? How would you comment on the Western judges?*

Z Y : It is hard to generate an answer with a few words. I do not speak English, so I do not think I am eligible to judge. Each person has his or her own point of view. However, if a jury likes a movie, this does not always mean that it is a good movie. It only reflects the view of the jury members. On the other hand, China is a developing country. The juries probably are curious about something they have never seen, something authentic, something that is hard to find in their society. The different living condition of each country defines how we see them and how they see us.

CW: *I made a comparison between your* Red Sorghum *and Chen Kaige's* Farewell My Concubine *and found an emphasis on symbolism and cultural content. Is it true that you are paying special attention to the symbolic content of the movies and intentionally convey such messages through your films?*

ZY: It is true. As I said, a work should be unique in idea. I think many Hollywood movies reflect a simple world outlook. Instead of putting emphasis on the breakthrough of the content, the symbolic aspect, they stress other entertainment elements to attract an audience, such as sensational approach and high technological skill. They carry a high price tag, and sometimes are very well done with love scenes and action. But in terms of artistic value, the symbolic meaning of the movies—some of them, not all—are kept plain. They may just draw lines of moral value, such as struggles between good and evil; something we are educated about once and for all in high school. I think movies should have more than just these; they should touch more varieties of the society, different aspects of life, and reflect people. They are more for development, more to explore. Of course this is only my personal view; each person may have their own view.

Zhang Yimou, Do You Have Any More Films

MUT YA / 1998

AFTER TWO YEARS OF silence, Zhang Yimou has finally cut his first "urban" film, *Keep Cool*, bringing together a huge alliance of stars such as Jiang Wen, Li Baotian, Liu Xinyi, Ge You, Li Xuejian, Fang Qingzhuo, and Zhao Benshan—not to mention Qu Ying, his new female lead following his parting with Gong Li. Moreover, due to all the media hype over the course of this film's production, the audience expects *Keep Cool* to be much more significant than the average exploratory film. Yet as this film is shown across the country, how will Zhang Yimou assess his own film? And how will he respond to the various expectations, disappointments, critical observations, and hopes toward his film? In response to all this, Zhang Yimou was happy to receive reporters in Wuhan. The reporter enjoyed this interview and offers it to our readers . . .

At one period of time, it seemed that your films were being produced for export. Domestic audiences could only "consume" your films one or two years after over-seas audiences, yet this actually created a demand for them—your films thus sold extremely well. This time, you've come out with particularly grand opening release ceremonies, and have even been accompanied by Jiang Wen, Li Baotian, and Qu Ying. Perhaps this is to pique people's curiosity?

Certainly. This is the second time I've held nation-wide release ceremonies since '82s [sic] *Red Sorghum*. My conducting them stems from several consid-erations: the first is that *Keep Cool* was made entirely through the investment

From *City Entertainment: Film Biweekly* No. 498 (14 May 1998). Reprinted by permission. Translated by Stephanie Deboer.

of domestic firms; the second is to assist our distribution company in domestic distribution; the third is also a desire to exchange and communicate a little with audiences—including students and you reporters—to see whether Chinese film is moving with the tide of current trends and is satisfying the needs of audience tastes.

In fact, you're also bringing this group to opening releases in order to promote sales. Could you tell us whether questions among you and your people about the distribution of profits have played into this? Do the earnings for this film seem very optimistic?

It's to promote sales. But it absolutely does not involve any problems between my people and me—the rights to distribute this film were bought by our distribution company for over ten million yuan. As for the present profits, they're quite sizable—in Beijing, it wasn't even four days after the first round of releases when the earnings already reached four million yuan—this could only be compared to a large imported film. You could even say that *Keep Cool* has brought vitality to the fatigued Chinese film market. The profits in such cities as Wuhan, Chengdu, Chongqing, Shenzhen, and Guangzhou haven't been insignificant.

One has to admit that, up to now, you've never made a film that lost money, but your previous films have all been rather artistic.

But I've also emphasized entertainment, plot, and dramatic qualities—demanded that they look good, that they're interesting. You should know that a director isn't the only creator and can't do whatever he or she wants. Against the many members of a production team—with all their input—it's irresponsible for a director to say that he or she alone made a film. We must at the very least get a return for investments.

The supporting roles for Keep Cool *include Li Xiejian, Fang Qingzhuo, and Zhao Benshan; you yourself also make a guest performance in a role as a junk collector. Was this done to pursue a star effect, or is it to court box offices due to the uncertainties of urban films?*

These big stars are all actors loved by the audiences. It certainly does also have the effect of box office appeal. Stars naturally have a presence onscreen. If conditions allow it, whenever I make a film from now on, I of course want to work with them, or with, say, other first-rate actors. As for my playing the role of a peasant junk collector, that was the result of a vote led by Jiang Wen and the rest of the cast. At that time, we hadn't yet found an actor to play that role, so I went through the scenes with Jiang Wen. The result of this was Jiang Wen insisting that if I didn't play the role, he wouldn't be able to get the right feeling. That's how I was pulled into the film.

You've said that this rural person speaking Shaanxi dialect and wearing army pants edged with red conforms to the mentality of the audience toward him as a character. I feel that the most brilliant part of the film is simply the scene in which you run like hell.

[He laughs.] Really? Actually, film acts as a kind of contemporary entertainment; while it tries to win the audience as much as possible, it also seems to hide—or rather disregard—its textual value. I feel that *Keep Cool* contains some seemingly careless and unemphasized surface-level depictions, the substance of which are actually painstakingly profound. It's difficult for film narrative to summarize this profundity simply.

This is what you've termed its "sense of fable"—you've said that Keep Cool *is essentially an urban fable. Could you explain a bit how it acts as a "filmic fable"?*

This "fable" comes from the screenwriter's commentary, and I think this characterization is extremely accurate. A fable is actually a kind of style, a kind of feeling. You can't directly or materially say what it symbolizes, or what it illustrates; you can't be sure that big historical events originate in incidental details or originate in certain patterns. The screenplay's most significant characteristic is its exaggeration of the absurdity of life—thus the film possesses a sense of irreversible absurdity and chance.

It's also to say, whether there's any interest in understanding another's portrait of the city within the turbulent and chaotic living environments of today—the hustle and bustle within which people can't find free time and rarely communicate with or understand one another.

Right. Each person has his or her own ideas and goals; urban life of today is extremely complicated—who can define modern life accurately, summarize it all? It can't be done. So I didn't want to—didn't have any way to—position the film on any particular point. I only hoped that it would be a film that would have a very strong sense of form, have a distinct personality, and give rise to all sorts of subjects.

Some people say that your films have become less and less equal to your previous ones, that they lack anything worth reflecting over, their feeling seemingly dried up. Take Keep Cool *for example. Except for the small comic "sketch" with you and Zhao Benshan and its exaggerated commercial effects, the rest seems to have very little feeling—this clamorous* Keep Cool *seems only suitable for middle school students. What's your opinion about all this?*

This has simply been the natural course of my creative process. Some people say that I stumbled from *Shanghai Triad* up to *Keep Cool*, that it' difficult to conceal my awkwardness in making this film! Actually, I'd had some plans from early on to make a contemporary urban film—I'd simply never realized them. The label doesn't really explain anything. There are two kinds of themes—those of historical or contemporary times. There are also two kinds of styles—the countryside or the city. Each has a fifty-fifty chance of possibility. So in the future, if I'm not able make a film because of insufficient funds, I could shoot about contemporary times instead of shooting about history—there's no other choice. In the future, I can be very flexible in my filmmaking. I many instances I will simply shoot what I have.

According to the publicity booklet, Keep Cool *is a film about "three men and a woman." But after seeing the film, many spectators felt that it's a bit more appropriate to call it "two men and a finger," because the majority of the film addresses this subject.*

Looking at it today, I think that the dining room scene was a little too long, and particular details were magnified too much for the audience to easily absorb. If we had cut three to five minutes, the effect would have been a little better. At the time, I simply wanted to depict the accidental meeting of two men, and its bringing about of a scene so often seen in the city—acts of violence for no particular reason with retaliation the motivation for the protagonists' actions. Later, Zhao Xiaoshuai's incidental act of retaliation—and not only the cracking ceiling or refrain from cutting Liu Delong's finger—was what drew Zhang Qiusheng into this kind of unexplainable circle of chance. Zhang Qiusheng also began to repeat the same incidental violence as Zhang Xiaoshuai in making his own acts of retaliation. Because of all this a scholar also became a fighter.

As for the question of the moving camera lens, even though you did it to approximate the clamor and turbulent feeling of the city, it still causes one to feel that your style and technique lacked control and didn't achieve what you expected—to create, in a wide angle lens, an expansive view that presents the desires of a few people of the city surviving its reality. Some critics frankly say that Keep Cool *is simply a reproduction of Wang Kar-wai's* Chungking Express. *What do you think about this?*

[Seems uncomfortable.] I still insist on what I've said about *Keep Cool*; its jumping lens is first related to its intrinsic idea—that urban life is much more turbulent than rural life, and this is also true for people's feelings. Second, the rhythm of the story itself is rather fast, its dramatic quality very strong, its audience intensity great and very compact—it suits this kind of form. Third, and most important, is that characters don't significantly communicate with one another, don't even have time to exchange names. There's no need for the camera lens to linger for long on people's faces. If the film were depicting a story of a complicated inner life, the audience would certainly demand that the lens remain on the actor's face so that they could appreciate the inner workings of the actor. The audience would be unsatisfied by the camera's moving away. The results of the theater showing today weren't bad—everyone was laughing, which goes to show that they understood what was being conveyed through the mobile lens, and that's enough. By the way, you didn't see this kind of style in the nineteen-thirties, forties, or fifties. What we see today in widespread MTV, in documentaries—revealed in all kinds of media—is what's been made new with the advancement of the times. As for copying Wang Kar-wai, that kind of criticism merely refers to its form or method—the contents are absolutely my own. But film must method and form; otherwise, you haven't made a film. The key to this is whether or not form and content are integrated—only one kind of form can effectively produce one kind of theme. I call this kind of form an "external model."

Many people, including us reporters, all want to ask the same question—does Zhang Yimou have any more films? The films you've made in the past have all taken international awards, but they've all have been about Chinese poverty and backwardness, resulting in an "Eastern spectacle" that pleases Westerners; this film, Keep Cool, *also seems to exhibit a suspicion of "the ugly Chinese." Your earlier films exposed the scars, ignorance, awkwardness, and provincialism of peasants. Your present* Keep Cool, *on the other hand, exhibits the ugliness of urban people—the fighting, the search for retaliation, the rough language. The group of*

old, thickly made-up women who danced yanko and sang hoarse, out of tune kara-
oke, for example, seemed hackneyed. As a result, you came back empty handed
from this year's Venice Film Festival—the judges indicated disappointment at your
manner of pursuing a bit of comic effect with little artistic exploration. It appears
that foreigners are also beginning to resent your custom of displaying "national
ugliness."

In places like Shenzhen and Guangzhou, I've also heard this line of question-
ing. To speak frankly, I really resent everyone's saying that I've been courting
foreign favor by making films that display "national ugliness"—this accusation has already been directed against my films for ten years, and I feel that
it's already a cliché. I don't agree with this because I've had exchanges with
many foreign figures over the past ten or more years—the people who say
that I'm trying to please foreigners have probably never left the country and
don't understand how films are evaluated overseas. There's no one in this
world that thinks this simply; rather there can be communication between
people, and you can't use such an insular theory to summarize everything.
As for the Venice Film Festival, I've always been of the opinion that the criterion for determining a good film doesn't lie in whether or not it wins a prize.
Moreover, the judges' objectives in making their public choice aren't necessarily the same from year to year. Let's take this year's Venice Film Festival—
nine judges came from eight different countries, nationalities, nations,
cultural backgrounds, and artistic tastes, resulting in a great sense of chance.
By chance, my first film about contemporary material didn't win an award,
but this doesn't prove that foreigners only like Chinese antiques, nor does it
prove that contemporary films can't be shot this way—it doesn't prove anything. But at film festival showings, *Keep Cool* was well received and praised
by the local media, and it really isn't like what the media in China has been
saying—that foreign countries liked it because it hadn't passed the censors.
Just because it doesn't pass the censors doesn't mean it will be well received.
There are over fifty film festivals in the world—if I wanted to win an award
every time I left the country, then I'd be exhausted. If it's in the hearts of the
audience, a good film doesn't really need an award to promote itself. Of
course, some younger directors see all this as important because it could fix
their place in the material world. If I were to say that I didn't care about any
award, then I'd be pretending a bit. The Cannes Film Festival is the largest
film festival in the world and has fifty years of history. *Farewell My Concubine*
fully deserved the first prize; I've only obtained the second prize, and I hope

that someday I can win the Palm d'Or. I'm often encouraged to compete in the Oscars. Many people hold the Oscars in such high esteem, it's a little ridiculous—in fact, this award is simply Americans judging their own country's or a few other English-speaking films. Although they have an award for best foreign picture, it's only a minor award, granted after the awards for shorts and documentaries. Moreover, films that compete for this award for best foreign picture each year must all be chosen and sent by their respective governments. Only when we no longer need awards from other countries will Chinese film really be strong.

Some people have said that you, Zhang Yimou, step on writers in order to stand up and direct, and others have said that the films you choose are nothing more than a continuation of Wang Shuo's "riffraff culture" or involve nothing more than love triangles. For example, the last embarrassing scene in which Zhang Qiusheng wears shorts—here's a Chinese intellectual pulled by the crowd and made into a lamb sacrificed to "comedy and humor." They also ask if mainstream life is really like this. To tell a good story, is it necessary to cram "boring love triangles" into a film to arouse feelings from the audience? There are also some that say they were surprised when Keep Cool *passed the censors because—even though it could take the box offices—the negative side effects of the film are too great.*

Many of the questions you bring up today make me angry. [He laughs.] The first thing I want to clearly say to you is that I don't care much about what others say, and I don't read periodicals or newspapers very often. Every once in a while when I see something about me, it will catch my interest and I'll read more, but I don't really pay attention to others' positive or negative views of me. This isn't to say that I stand aloof; I've become this way because it's difficult to cater to all tastes—people will have all sorts of attitudes toward my work. As for standing on writers, this really is a stupid question. It goes without saying that literature and film have both similar and different modes of appreciation. Good literary works are the solid foundation of film; on the other hand, film can also enrich literature. Why doesn't somebody say that I, Zhang Yimou, have made a few writers successful? Of course, it also has to do with the fame of the writers themselves. This subject is too big to talk about; it involves anything from my country's lack of screenwriters to questions of the quality of screenwriters. The male/female romantic relationship is a long-standing theme; the key lies in how it's put to use in the film— whether it conforms to things like the qualities of the characters, the style of the film, and levels of audience identification. Film form originates from life. As for the question of passing the censors, this should be attributed to reforms of the film system—"let a hundred flowers blossom and a hundred schools of thought contend," right? To tell the truth, *Keep Cool* was the most smoothly passed film in my ten years of directing. As film and TV reporters, you should understand this. I feel that making films domestically is really more difficult than making them abroad. Others only need to solve problems of money—they don't have any ideological problems. My creative space is not very wide, so I'm very concerned about the level of openness in Chinese reform measures, as well as a loose atmosphere for subject matter. Right now, I have only one wish: whenever I have the chance to make a film, that the conditions will be available to me to make it well.

Over the past few years, I've noticed that you've said at several public occasions that "repetition is a kind of stupidity." I've observed that over the past two years your films have shown signs of change, and Jiang Wen has told me that your films have "become more profound." Have you also felt this? Do you have any enlightening remarks on the trends of film at the end of this century?
China pays attention to established rules, emphasizes order and artistic method, isn't expert in richness of color, or variety and change. Once a director has made a few films, people begin to use a ruler to measure you and summarize all your work as "X" model. There aren't too many film forms in China at the present; rather, there are too few, the contents reflected are too limited, and there aren't many films with character. I've made films for over ten years and have already reached that age when people look for security and a so-called masterly style. *Keep Cool* has an obvious sense of experimentalism and risk—it's like a student's composition exercise. There are probably people who say that it isn't as complete or substantial as my past films, but I value the vitality of this work. Let's sit down and really talk about this film. When I was in Guangzhou, a reporter told me that I carefully analyzed only the strong points of my film and was vague about its weak points. For now I will, as much as possible, try to keep my creative approach at an ordinary level and work hard to overcome my fixed ways of thinking, treat myself as a white piece of paper, and urge myself to lay down moral and mental burdens in making films—always find things that excite me. The most important impulse of a creative work is its emotional impulse. *Yellow Earth* was well received because it revealed Chen Kaige's true feelings. *Shanghai Triad* didn't

succeed—in the end it relied on factors such as monetary investment and societal concerns that forced me to make something I didn't love. A film's vitality and personality is very important. I don't like uninspired, overcautious popular goods very much. Therefore, I say that repetition is a kind of stupidity—the process of not repeating allows people to be infatuated with what they do. There are only three years from now to the end of the twenty-first century, and I feel that there won't be a significant change in Chinese film. The development of Chinese film still has a long way to go. We of this generation are also the pavers of Chinese film's brilliant future—we are a part of this process. I feel that Chinese film is a part of Chinese culture, and only once the country is powerful will we be able to truly give expression to it. Earlier, I brought up the Oscars. No matter how you say it, the whole world knows about it. An audience of several hundred million watches this one prize-giving ceremony. I was expressing concern for American film's powerful cultural invasion throughout the world. Even as I call for the Chinese government's opening up of the Chinese film market, we must also pay attention to protecting the fragile foundation of Chinese film products. I've been to many countries in Europe, including those old film countries such as France and Italy. When they talk with you it's all about how to resist American films and how to protect the development of native film. Our own film market also hasn't yet completely opened up—only ten so-called big pictures come in each year. To tell the truth, if our market were to completely open up and allow American film to flood in, the Chinese film industry could collapse after not even a year. I think that our mission before the world is to resist the cultural invasion of American imperialism. [He laughs.]

Compared to the past when people swarmed to make historical films, films with urban themes have assumed a rising trend in the last few years. Yet they've received very few awards, including the domestic Hundred Flowers and Golden Rooster awards as well as big awards in overseas film festivals. This is also true for your Keep Cool. *It seems that it's very difficult to bring urban films to maturity.* This statement is arbitrary. There indeed are not many excellent urban films. But what still needs some clarification is that no matter who's made an urban film, no director would dare to say that his or her urban film is the true reflection of urban life because this would be an exaggeration. I'll emphasize again, what *Keep Cool* reflects is nothing more than a corner of city life. Here, we should think about the literature of China; it's relationship with Chinese

film and television is very close. If we think about it carefully, Chinese literature of the '80s flourished, had depth, width, and dynamism; because of this,
it influenced the film and television of the time very deeply, and many films
were adapted from fiction. But up until now, I can say that today's film and
television culture still hasn't taken shape. I'm answering again what you
brought up about my so-called directorial issue of "standing on writers"—
I'm based in this environment. Our urban culture has received Western influence, including all kinds of philosophies and research on postmodernism.
The "contamination" from the West is very deep—wearing western clothes,
smoking western cigarettes, speaking western languages, learning the customs of westerners, often using the standards of the west to measure ourselves. Until we form a distinctive Chinese urban culture, our urban films
can't be powerful because we're still characterized as "local products." Because we still need to go through a process, only once we've reached a point
where China's urban culture plays a "leading role" in the world can films
about urban themes—or the Chinese film industry—truly stand up bold and
assured.

I feel that Hong Kong and Taiwanese films about the city have been better at at-
tracting audiences than those of the mainland. Maybe this is because you had a
special relationship with Gong Li at the time, so in several of the Hong Kong films
that Gong Li participated in, you lent your services as a supervisor, etc. May I ask
what you think about Hong Kong and Taiwanese films?
I must admit that the quality of people in Hong Kong and Taiwan is higher
than that of the mainland. In all sorts of aspects such as education and cultural influence, they are different from the mainland. But as for Hong Kong
and Taiwanese films, I don't like them. What I don't like is the feeling that
those kinds of films are made to make you laugh, and once they've amused
you it's over—this isn't our way of going about it. When making a film,
surely there are many things you want to express—this goes without saying.
Of course, having reached the 1990s, film must first of all cause the audience
to want to watch it, due to the demands of a market economy.

Everyone understands that China's present film market is in a worrisome situation.
Managers of movie theaters are all condemning Chinese films—both outstanding
and inferior national films—but I feel that what they're really condemning is the
audience who, inexplicably, only likes "big imported films." Also, if there's no re-

sult at the box office, all the praise from experts has no meaning—no matter how enthusiastic their artistic probing, they never judge a movie by the box office. Therefore, people also doubt what the critics say.

What causes me to really sigh sometimes is how difficult it is to "wait upon" the audience. If we made today the *Yellow Earth* of over ten years ago, the artistic quality would be the same, but it's uncertain whether the majority of spectators would want to go see it, so filmmaking must also adapt to the demands of the times. Our present goal in making a film is to both attract an audience but never forfeit the self—this is important. In Guangzhou, one reporter said that the fifth generation didn't finish too early or end too late but appropriately passed away after flourishing for ten years; the reporter also said they were pleased by the emergence of sixth generation directors. In Shenzhen there was even a reporter who said that we could call *Keep Cool* a "seventh generation" film. Having lead the way of the fifth generation, for me to step over two generations and once again take a leading position in a new wave of film is worthy of some arrogance. This is all contradictory and leaves me confused.

I think this is to indicate its avoidance of cultural and moral missions, evasion and abstraction of reality and history, and disregard of solicitude for a national spirit; this is perhaps an annotation to this "passing away." However, sixth generation films such as Dirt *pleasantly surprised us. You, Zhang Yimou, could also claim to be the figure no one else can topple. The flag you carry no longer carries the same prestige, yet we can't say that no one of the sixth or seventh generation doesn't want to run laboriously after you to capture it.*

I still say the same thing: we of this generation are the pavers of Chinese film's brilliant future—we are part of this process. We could also work according to Chairman Mao's quotation, "Don't rely upon prestige to make a new contribution." We all know, too, that if you harbor a certain kind of style for a long time your work could become self-indulgent. Even if you say that I've expressed something really great, it's still useless. Today's audience buys movie tickets spontaneously—there's no order from above to see *Keep Cool*, for example. The first thing we had to consider when making the film was how to attract an audience. Sometimes we also confront what you've just said—the significance of a film belongs to audience reception and not to critical or artistic enthusiasm. So we don't pay attention to such phrases as the fifth or sixth or seventh generation.

According to recent news, Jiang Wen left the production of The Emperor's Assassin *after having a dispute with Chen Kaige. During* Keep Cool, *did you and Jiang Wen run into any situations in which you had to "keep cool"? It's also been said that Jiang Wen isn't an easy master to wait upon; was having Jiang Wen stutter a good way of producing a good character?*

What I can tell you is that Jiang Wen and I are good friends. Ten years ago we worked very happily together on *Red Sorghum*. I think that it's normal to have discussions, and in business, talk about business. When we make films, the topic of conversation is, of course, often film because it possesses qualities of art, entertainment, or education, doesn't it? As a result, it's not easy to make a good film, and questions about a film's plot, characters, or setting are all open to question and debate. This is beneficial to the creation of a film.

I should say that working with Jiang Wen has been a good experience. Moreover, to tell the truth, the strength of this film really lies in the brilliant performances of Jiang Wen, Li Baotian, Qu Ying, and other big star contributors. In Wuhan one reporter asked, "If *Keep Cool* hadn't collected this 'heroic bundle of fire wood,' could its 'flame' have been so high?" I rather agree with this phrase. I've already said at the beginning that this film contains elements of star effect. If they'd completely followed the screenplay without displaying their personalities and their brilliant understandings of their roles, I'm afraid there wouldn't be so much laughter. You could say that the places where the audience laughed today all depended on the comedic background of the performers; the director couldn't tell them every instruction to follow. Actually, it's extremely difficult to act in this kind of film because the jumping camera will press this close and force the performers to utilize their full talent—only highly skilled performers could perform in this kind of film. So the contribution of these main actors was great, and they all worked very well together.

As for Jiang Wen's stammer, Jiang Wen himself thought up this performance method. Its purpose was to distinguish the two characters, Zhao Xiaoshuai and Zhang Qiusheng—to contrast their manners of linguistic expression. Because Zhang Qiusheng is a person who speaks very fast, when the two speak together, one talks on and on forever and the other speaks irritatingly slow. This is what made up the dramatic quality of the plot. Also, in real life, Jiang Wen also stammers a little when he's anxious.

Some reports say that Hou Yaohua said that your films turn their actors into props, so he would never act in your films. Qu Ying's character of An Hong in Keep Cool *also seems to be a prop. And this is similar to your leading this crew to release ceremonies—people like Jiang Wen, Li Baotian, and Qu Ying are all like your "foils" because everyone comes for you and most often directs questions at you.*

Did Hou Yaohua say that? I've met him several times, and never heard him say this. The early fifth generation films certainly had particular tendencies, yet I basically changed in later films—Hou Yaohua probably hasn't seen my recent films. In any case, internationally speaking, every year will have a few films that turn the actors into props—this could be called one kind of film style. [At this time, Li Baotian to the side, can't help but add some strong words: people who say this, first, would say that grapes are sour because they can't reach them; second, I've made films with Zhang Yimou three times—I have the right to say whether Zhang Yimou turns actors into props.] As for these release ceremonies, to say that people like Jiang Wen, Li Baotian, and Qu Ying are only my foils is a little inappropriate. Everyone knows everything about them—has been acquainted with them for a long time—so I'm essentially the target of all questions, since I don't often show my face.

When you decided to use Qu Ying in Keep Cool, *it was really big news. How do you feel about her performance in the film? Have you passed on to Qu Ying the leading female role in all your future films? After Gong Li, are you thinking again about developing another international star like Gong Li?*

I've answered this question over a hundred times—beginning from Beijing each place has had someone ask this—but I'm still happy to answer it. Everyone knows what's happened in the past, so I won't talk about that. In China, filmmaking still doesn't rely on the star system in which screenplays are planned to revolve around a particular star, but rather we choose an actor after having seen a good script. Qu Ying is a good actress. If in the future I see a good script that has a character that suits her, I think I could ask her to work with me again. But as for comparing Qu Ying and Gong Li, I feel there's no way to compare the two—they are simply two types of actresses. It's just like Jiang Wen and Li Baotian, each with his or her own style and personality—can you say who's better?! There's no way to compare them—it's like trying to compare apples and oranges. I feel that An Hong's life is similar to Qu Ying's—it has to do with her character, her profession. She in many ways embodies the modern urban girl—average with a rather Western flavor and

strong modern sense. If I were to make Qu Ying play a country girl, she could
hardly do it! And stars don't entirely depend upon development. Gong Li
has become a star as a result of her own abilities; if she had no ability, then
all the praise of all the directors in China couldn't make her into a star. It's
also true that there aren't very many actors around today with potential talent—we're facing a temporary shortage. Up to today, there still hasn't been
anyone to truly challenge the best actors of China such as Jiang Wen and Li
Baotian—there's no one who can topple them. A director's discovery and
promotion is one aspect, yet for actors the most important is whether or not
they have the right stuff.

*The last question: Do you have any more films? I'm referring to any plans you
might have for your next film. How are preparations for Wu Zetian? Will Gong Li
still play the lead?*
[He laughs]. Thank heaven there's only one question left. I'm now putting
together screenplays—both historical ones and contemporary ones—but
they still haven't taken shape. Right now I have the money and the people
but lack a script. Everyone knows that shooting a film according to a script
in China really isn't easy. Sometimes you don't have a choice in what you
shoot. I'm overly picky about screenplays; the script for *Keep Cool* was revised
so many times, and it had about seven or eight hundred thousand Chinese
characters. This is because you have to consider passing the concerned units;
you must also consider the tastes of investors and audiences and only third
can you consider questions of the right kinds of male and female leads to
express the director's personality. As for the preparations for making *Wu Zetian*, we're still at the stage of revising the script. We'd already agreed a few
years ago with investors and the shooting company that Gong Li would perform in it—generally speaking, this can't be changed. By the way, there are
no obstacles to speak of to prevent me and Gong Li from working on a film
together.

*Thank you for patience in talking with us. We also thank you for taking the time
out of your busy schedule to interview with us.*
What I face are audiences, and what you face are readers—the nature of our
work can be said to be the same, so let's understand and support each other.
To tell the truth, the work of us filmmakers depends upon the dissemination
of film critics like you. We rely on you and should thank you.

Zhang Yimou: No Going Back

YEUNG WAI-LAN/1999

''LET'S WAIT UNTIL I'VE eaten to have the interview.''
"Sure, sure."
"There's nowhere to sit. Do you mind squatting while we talk?
"No problem."
A straightforward man of few words, Zhang Yimou seems accustomed to speaking with strangers about his films at any time and place.

True and False Documentaries

Not One Less *brings to mind* The Story of Qiu Ju. *For that film, you first used an unloaded camera to "shoot" the townspeople. Only after they'd gotten used to the camera's presence did you load it with film and get hidden footage—by this time they no longer gazed at the camera lens. The effect of this was quite realistic and was very inspiring to documentary filmmakers.*
The documentary component of *Not One Less* is greater than that of *Qiu Ju*. The latter still used professional actors, and only employed hidden filming techniques to enhance the film's sense of reality. The demands for *Not One Less* have been even more rigorous. All the actors are originally from the professions they play in the film.

Chinese film and television often use the word "real" as their catch phrase, yet the things they produce are extremely false—especially those so-called "documentary" or "news" TV programs.

From *City Entertainment: Film Biweekly*, No. 501 (25 June 1999). Reprinted by permission. Translated by Stephanie Deboer.

This question is very simple. There are good and bad documentaries, and the ones you've seen have been poorly made. In mainland television stations over the last few years, some documentary programs—including CCTV's *In Focus*—have been pretty well made and have exposed some societal problems. You can see that they've improved.

In the end, no matter what type of film you make, what's most important is not to preach—not to openly educate or force your views on your audience. Instead, through particular details, allow your viewers to experience your subject for themselves. I would say that this rule applies to every art. I think that education should also reflect these aims.

Elementary School Ties

I've heard that your subject matter this time was adapted from a story in a Xinjiang literary magazine.
Right, I came upon this story by chance. But actually, I've always been interested in elementary school students. This sentiment can really be traced back to 1984's *Yellow Earth*. At that time, we ran everywhere up and down the Yellow River to choose shot locations in the countryside.

I found that almost every village had an elementary school. We'd hear the sound of lessons being read aloud and immediately know that there was one nearby. We'd always go there to take a look. We sometimes saw schools that had only a few children. In such a poor environment, they were studying the most rudimentary knowledge. We'd hear them read aloud the text, which explained all kinds of vocabulary like "ocean" and "mountain," but they probably didn't understand what they were and would probably never see them.

These scenes have left a deep impression on me for these past ten years. I can't explain why, but every time I go to a new place that has an elementary school, I'll always go and take a look. Shooting a story about a mountain village elementary school has actually been my dream for many years.

No Going Back

In June of last year, you directed the opera, Turandot, *in Beijing, and this summer you'll direct a new one. As a film director, do you think you are equal to directing operas?*
There's no reason to worry about this; I was quite satisfied with last year's performance. This year on 5 September, the opera I am directing will open

in the Forbidden City, and the opening ceremonies are set to be held in front of the main hall of E Fang palace.

After this opera, I plan to begin shooting my next film, *The Road Home*, which is also a story that takes place in a contemporary mountain village. After that, *Not One Less* and *The Road Home* should both be finished by next spring.

"Ignorant and Ill Informed"

Whenever I run into mainland directors at foreign film festivals, I always see them working hard to see as many films as possible. You've all come into contact with so many foreign films overseas; have they inspired you in any specific way?
The films we mainland directors are able to see are still too limited. I really envy Hong Kong directors—their homes are full of so many VCDs, laser discs, videotapes! And arranged so carefully—Kurosawa Akira, Coppola . . .

We mainland directors can't come close to this—I certainly can't either. First of all, I don't understand any foreign languages, so I can't understand many original versions. I can only collect those with Chinese subtitles, but these films are usually distributed through Hong Kong and Taiwanese business networks. If they don't buy a film, they don't distribute or create subtitles for it. So even if I watch it, I still don't understand.

Second, we still don't have the ability or channels through which to collect many films. When I go overseas, I can see twenty films in ten days. In addition to this, I've figured that in one month in mainland China, I'm doing pretty well if I see an average of two foreign films. I'm talking about new releases; older films are of course very difficult to view here. In a word, we don't have these kinds of conditions.

When we filmmakers go abroad, by and large we all see a few things, but there really are limits. So the influence on us from foreign films is sometimes great and sometimes insignificant. This just depends on the particular person.

Strictly speaking, we are comparatively ignorant and ill informed. We don't understand the rest of the world very well. For instance, you see a certain movie and you immediately think, "Wow! This film is great!" From this moment on, it deeply affects you, and then you later imitate this film without being aware of it. This is one kind of influence.

On the other hand, say you're able to see very few films and in any case don't know what they're all about. You just don't think in the same way—

they are them and you are you. You decide to shoot according to your own ideas and not to think about whether your film resembles the work of this or that person. As much as possible, I hope to achieve this latter kind of film-making.

Sometimes, once I've made a film, a reporter will expertly ask me if I've seen this or that director's film. He or she is actually saying that this film of yours is very similar to that person's and haven't you been influenced by him or her. Or else they'll ask, who is your favorite foreign director, when in fact they're all trying to coax out of me the source of my creation. But for me, none of this exists. I haven't seen many of the films they bring up because we see so few. And I generally make films on the basis of my own experiences and interests. Of course, you could bring up some movies that correspond to what we've seen, but on the whole, we aren't really influenced by them.

Survival over Value

Is your current method of choosing and considering themes the same as it's been in the past?

Of course. I still first consider whether or not a film will be approved—this is a question that's always existed. When you make a film in China, you will definitely confront it. It's about survival. First is survival, and only next is artistic value. If you can't survive, then where does this value come from? If you can't shoot, then isn't it a waste of time to talk about it? It's useless!

From the Fifth to the Sixth Generation: An Interview with Zhang Yimou

TAN YE / 1999

T HE COLOR RED IS the signature for most of Zhang Yimou's films—red sorghum (*Red Sorghum*), red silk (*Ju Dou*), red lantern (*Raise the Red Lantern*), red dress (*The Story of Qiu Ju*), and so on. All sensuous, all symbolic. Classical Chinese theater is full of color symbols: a red face suggests loyalty; a black face, bravery; and a white face, evil. New China inherited some old color symbolism and created some new color symbols, among which red is by far the most important. It is the color of revolution: red flags, little red books, Red Guards, and of course the red sun, which is the symbol of Chairman Mao. But what does Zhang Yimou's red suggest? Some commentators liken the red setting sun at the end of *Red Sorghum* to a Japanese national flag: some think the red lanterns in *Raise the Red Lantern* reveal the sexual dominance of the patriarchal despot—but the setting sun would also have been used to elegize the perished heroine and the red lanterns may also connote the fulfillment of the concubine's desire. Zhang Yimou's red color, like his other symbols, defies narrow interpretation because it is at once an inheritance from and is rebellion against tradition. Red is no longer simply a color of celebration in old China or a color of revolution as in modern China, nor is it a color of malice. Perhaps it should be treated as a mood. As Zhang Yimou once said, "We Chinese have been too moderate, too reserved . . . the boundless red of sorghum fields arouses sensory excitement . . . it encourages unrestrained lust for life."

From *Film Quarterly*, vol. 53, no. 2 (Winter 1999–2000). © 2000 by The Regents of the University of California.

Lust for life was restrained in China, a fact Zhang Yimou knows all too well. He had a miserable childhood: his father was a Nationalist officer, hence a "bad element"; his mother was a medial doctor, not a good element either. When the Cultural Revolution broke out, he was sent to the country to be "reeducated" by peasants. Then he became a porter. Red to him is the primary color of life—symbolically, realistically, and artistically. While still unable to earn enough food, Zhang Yimou sold his blood to buy his first camera. It was the pictures he took with that camera that won him the opportunity to study cinematography at Beijing Film Academy in 1978.

After graduation, Zhang Yimou became known as the best cameraman in China: *Yellow Earth* (1984), a film he made with another Fifth Generation director, Chen Kaige, won eleven international awards. In 1986 he played a peasant in Wu Tianming's *Old Well*, which brought him the title of best actor at the 1987 Tokyo International Film Festival and the opportunity to make his own film. His directing debut, *Red Sorghum*, was awarded the Golden Bear at the Berlin Film Festival in 1988. Two years later, his *Ju Dou* received the Luis Buñuel Award at the Cannes Film Festival. At the 1992 Venice Film Festival with the *Story of Qiu Ju*, Zhang Yimou received the Golden Lion. Since *Yellow Earth*, Zhang Yimou's films have won more than forty awards. His most recent work, *Not One Less (Yige ye buneng shao)*, which is about a young teacher's efforts to keep students from cutting class in a poor village school, took the top prize at the 1999 Venice Film Festival. This was the same film that was so misunderstood by the committee of the Cannes Film Festival that Zhang Yimou withdrew it from the festival. If we realize post-Tiananmen Square censorship is still hanging over Chinese filmmakers' heads, we will come to appreciate not only Zhang's artistic talent but also his talent as a political strategist.

No contemporary Chinese film is totally free of political messages. They are either imposed by the authorities or implied by the artist. For those who are interested in this kind of message, Zhang's color red does carry one. But contrary to what many critics say, it may not be purely political. Sick of Chairman Mao's theory and practice of "class struggle," all the Fifth Generation directors try not to be obtrusively political. Zhang Yimou's red is rather a commemoration of freedom, exuberance, and the most primal desires and aspirations, which have been denied by both Confucianism and Communism.

Most of Zhang Yimou's films speak for the downtrodden and the rebellious. *Red Sorghum* glorifies the elopement of a winery owner's wife with a sedan carrier; *Ju Dou* supports an affair between a worker and his boss's wife; *Raise the Red Lantern* sides with four concubines and treats their husband as a villain; *The Story of Qiu Ju* praises an ordinary peasant woman for her courage to sue the village chief; *To Live* attributes the misery of a meek family to the power struggle between Communists and Nationalists; *Shanghai Triad* sympathizes with a singer whose life is owned by an underworld magnate in pre—revolutionary Shanghai. And *Keep Cool* (*Youhoua haohao shuo*) (1996) empathizes with losers in love and career in the commercialized Beijing of the 1990s.

It is no surprise that some of Zhang's films are still banned in China. Equipped with the theory of socialist realism, some Chinese critics denounced his work for being "untrue to history." Although their real criticisms were leveled at Zhang's unorthodox treatment of humanity rather than this untruthful reflection of history, those critics' historical observations were quite accurate: no matter how many concubines a feudal lord possessed, he would never put up red lanterns to announce which one he favored on any particular night. Red lanterns were raised only when he was honored by the emperor as a moral paragon. What Zhang Yimou attempts to glorify is not orthodox history, and certainly not official paragons, but humanity caught in history. If his films are historically untrue, they are nevertheless universally true because in them we find the same pathos as in, say, *Oedipus Rex*, *Ghosts*, and *Desire Under the Elms*. In the following interview, Zhang Yimou refuses to be categorized into any school, but he does admit that his style is characteristic of the Northern Chinese. "I love the strong and the trenchant," meaning the color red in his films.

TAN YE: *Your early films rebelled in both form and content; is it true that your rebellion was mainly against three things: hypocritical political preaching, the mediocrity of the contemporary films, and traditional culture?*

ZHANG YIMOU: This was not very clear. To be honest with you, we artists do not contemplate that many theoretical issues. When we started making films more than ten years ago, we definitely wanted to rebel. Defiance against the older generation is born with the younger generation. The same youthful defiance exists in other walks of life too. This is also true with the Sixth Generation's rebellion.[1] It is not clear whether the rebellion is against politics, or art forms, or art content, or older generations, of traditional aesthetics. In

154 ZHANG YIMOU: INTERVIEWS

art, creative impulse plays a bigger role than theory. As for rebellion, frankly, I did not have at theoretical target.

Among all the Fifth Generation directors, you are the least didactic. Chen Kaige[2] and Tan Zhuangshuang[3] are relatively more philosophical.
This is because I have my own understanding of the nature of film. I think film originated from various folk performances. It should be very common and popular. I don't think a film should carry too much theory. After all, it is not philosophy or a concept to be taught in a classroom.

Although when making *Yellow Earth* as a cameraman, I had to help Kaige realize his subject, when making *Red Sorghum* by myself, I preferred to make it more appealing to the senses. I tend to believe that films are about emotions. An artist's ideas should be understood naturally through emotions. I think the subject matter of a film should be simple. Only after it is simplified, after the thoughts are simplified, can the capacity and power of emotions [of a film] be strengthened. If the subject matter and thoughts are too complicated, emotions will definitely be weakened. It would be like writing an essay with abstract symbols. It is a different kind of film. There are films like that, but I do not like them. Kaige prefers more thoughtful themes. His difference may have something to do with our personalities.

Your cinematography contributed a great deal to the achievement of Yellow Earth.
In making a film, none of the crew can be left out. Understand Chen Kaige's style. We are friends and know each other well. I know that he wants to reveal his heartfelt philosophy. You can treat *Yellow Earth* as a nonrealistic film, an auteur film. If I know that the director wants to make an auteur film, I will surely express his ideas accordingly with my camera.

You often use extreme shots. You said, when making One and Eight (Yige be bage),[4] *that you would never repeat shots used previously by other cameramen. You very consciously applied technique to artistic creation. Isn't that also a kind of rebellion?*
That kind of rebellion had its contemporary target, but would not last forever. That was when the Gang of Four[5] was just overthrown. Chinese films were very rigid; they could not escape from the shadow of previous taboos. Therefore, in such simple matters as the form of filmic expression and how to make a film, there were often very doctrinal and rigid ideas, which we

thought were outdate and stupid. So *One and Eight* was a rebellion against such stupidity, against affectation, pretense, and artificiality. But that kind of rebellion directed toward a specific phenomenon is rarely seen in China today. Rebellion is no longer a purpose but a story or theme.

We look for an appropriate way to tell a story according to its subject matter. In other words, what happens in China is not a purposeful rebellion targeted to a specific form. Actually, *One and Eight* is not that original and its characterization not that outstanding. It was a simple rebellion in filmic form.

When Chen Kaige was adapting Ming ru qinxian[6] *for his film* Life on a String, *I felt that his philosophy overshadowed his story. He seemed to realize it afterwards with* Farewell My Concubine. *But* Temptress Moon . . . ?
We all love *Farewell My Concubine.* When making *Temptress Moon*, Kaige was interviewed by a journalist and he said that *Temptress Moon* would be even better. I, however, feel that *Temptress Moon* went back to his old stubborn way. I am not sure about the quality of his new film, *The First Emperor (Jin Ke ci Quin)*. Maybe this is what makes Kaige; this is his own filmic world.

After all these changes, is the Fifth Generation still a unified group?
No, not anymore.

Historically, what was the achievement of the Fifth Generation? Was it mainly a breakthrough?
I think so. From a pragmatic perspective, this breakthrough attracted the attention of audiences. From an aesthetic or pure filmic perspective, our achievement was also a breakthrough. We can now regard it as the snow of yesteryear—now we can watch foreign films everywhere (including thousands of pirated tapes). But in those years, in the 1980s, information did not travel fast; therefore, in general, the Chinese were quite close-minded then. That presented a historical possibility. If the same thing happened in present-day China, the impact of the breakthrough would not be easily felt. If a good film came out yesterday, by today everyone has seen it. Can you surpass this?

Compared with foreign films, what do you think of Chinese films nowadays?
I think Chinese filmmakers have to work hard; otherwise, we will lag behind.

The time of the glorious rise of Chinese films is over. Especially in the 1990s, Asian films are becoming very strong. Films made in Iran, Japan, and Korea are quite good. I like Iranian films particularly. We should also include films made in Hong Kong and Taiwan. In the past we looked down on Taiwan films. Now the situation is totally different. Ang Lee and John Woo are making films in Hollywood. Wong kar Wai's films also have good artistic merits.

No matter what, directors in mainland China cannot brag anymore; we cannot say with confidence that we are representative of Asian cinema or Oriental cinema. Also, the whole world is moving very fast and making films in China is becoming very difficult. For instance, the Sixth Generation cannot catch up; they do not have any outstanding work. Furthermore, the political and economic conditions in China have worsened. So, all Chinese directors, old and young, have to work hard. If we don't, all the glory will be gone with the past. Out time will be over. Certainly, there will be occasional good works, but we will not be talked about; we will not be the focus of attention.

Granted that you now have to consider the market as well as art, you still present something original in each new film. Is it true that, after the completion of each film, you always want to revitalize yourself with a new style in the next film?
It is probably true. Among the Fifth Generation my style is the most changeable. My films are totally unrelated. They run in all directions. They lack a consistent style. Kaige is more consistent; he searches for the stately and philosophical; his shots are contrived for enduring strength. Relatively speaking, Zhuanzhuang's ideas are vague. I myself tend to experiment with all kinds of things. Sometimes the sheer change of style will excite me.

All these changes have made your personal style rather obscure. For this reason, some foreign critics find it hard to trace your style; possibly some domestic critics feel the same?
It is hard to fit me into a standardized pattern indeed. Maybe two of my films will fit a certain pattern, but the third does not. Critics in China feel the same. They said that my *Keep Cool* perplexed them. None of them could figure it out. *Keep Cool* is perhaps the most talked-about film in China with all kinds of opinions. Actually I love this. I like to stir up the pond. To me, the excitement of stirring up the water is greater than that of receiving the audiences' praises.

Some people said that you could not film urban life. Is Keep Cool *an answer to them?*

Not necessarily. There has been talk about my inability to make a film about urban life for years. With this film I only wanted to contradict myself, to extend my flexibility. It is a challenge to change from the country to the city, from epic and august styles to playful, relaxed, and MTV styles. I am planning to make a film about city life, one about country life, and one about history. If I make anther film about city life, it will definitely be different from *Keep Cool.*

Keep Cool sold extremely well at home but not so internationally. Of course, the promotional strategy was not efficient. It did not sell as well as my previous films, and the international reviews were not so favorable. For sure, there has been some noise domestically too. This was definitely a risk, I realized this when many foreign film companies came to see the film. It is like selling cloisonné: for many years, ten carts full of cloisonné had a market guaranteed for ten cart loads. If you suddenly replace cloisonné with lacquer tea cups the merchants dare not buy them. "OK, leave them here for the moment." Thus, a deal cannot be reached. In many countries, the audience never had a chance to see this film because the merchants never bought it. "Since this is a film made by Zhang Yimou," a foreign merchant would think, "I should not offer a low price because I do not want to be disrespectful. But if you want me to pay the same price as for his previous films, I dare not because this is not the type I am used to. I am unsure of the market."

This time it was very bad. Many of the merchants who previously bought many of my films were dubious after the screening. It is definitely risky—the more you appear unpredictable, the more problematic you become to market. Nevertheless, film critics are happy about it because it provides them with a new topic. I am willing to run such risks. If there are people who are willing to fund me, and I do not have to worry too much about money, why shouldn't I take the opportunity?

You said that you chose Qu Ying[7] because of her modernity. Are you becoming more modernized?

Not necessarily, I chose her because her image matched the story.

In general, what do you think of Chinese actors?

Uneven. There are good ones, but most of them are unqualified.

Reading your notes about cinematography for Yellow Earth, *one can tell you like traditional arts, especially traditional Chinese paintings.*
Yes, I love painting. I also love traditional theory on painting, but I have not accomplished much in painting. In Italy [the summer of 1997 when Zhang was directing the opera *Turandot*] we borrowed a great deal from Chinese classical aesthetics and principles on painting. We turned theory into reality.

It seems you prefer the bold and expressionistic school [xieyi] to the delicate and detailed one [gongbi]?
That's right. I am no good with delicate substance. So my films, including *Keep Cool*, may have different styles and emotions, but toward the end of my life, when I have finished filmmaking, all my hundreds of changes can be unified as characteristic of Northern Chinese. That is, I love the strong and the trenchant. *Keep Cool* is very strong. If its second half could have been done my way, I could have made this film much better. Unfortunately, we were not allowed to do that. Originally, *Keep Cool* was divided into two parts. It was like driving a car from the east, then reversing to the west. You are first made to believe it was cheerful, foolish horseplay, but after the turn, the heroine disappears and towards the end it becomes black humor. The story could have been very interesting, but there was no way we could do it freely. Even the present version was almost censored.

My next film is entitled *Going to Beijing Immediately (Mashang jing Beijing)*. I am not sure whether I can get it made. I intend it to be a Chinese highway film where all shots show movements. Many of them are on trains, buses, and taxis. At this stage, I am still trying to find the best way to do it. I think this film should have many meanings. Unlike foreigners, Chinese people don't drive a car on the highway. Even though I drive a jeep, the majority of the Chinese are definitely unable to do so. Therefore, I want to catch glimpses of Chinese people's lives. It is a certain kind of visual language that I hope to apply to filmmaking. It should not mere decoration. Before every film, I try seriously to grasp such a visual language. Unless I have found it, I cannot make a film.

As He Saifei[8] mentioned, you work not only conscientiously but also collectively. Very often you invite opinions from your crew.
This can be said as one of my merits. If there is anything I cannot handle, I

will invite people to chat with me. Only during the discussions can I find inspiration. It has become a habit of mine.

Apart from learning through practice and watching films made by others, do you have time to improve yourself through other means?
It is not that I am too busy to do anything else. I saw a ballet the day before yesterday. And I am always reading. All kinds of books, even trashy books, magazines, and papers. I read whatever I can lay my hands on—mostly novels. I subscribe to more than thirty magazines. All of them are fiction; I rarely read theory.

You said that freshness in your work excites you. Your Ju Dou *and* Raise the Red Lantern *were fresh to many people, particularly to Westerners. For this reason some Chinese critics said that you were creating "Orientalism" to please foreigners. Also, in your first films, the leading roles were mainly female; some other critics thus said you were a "feminist," but I don't think that was accurate either because traditionally in Chinese theater, female characters have more appeal to the audience.*
Right. It was neither orientalism nor feminism. All that was not deliberately designed. There is a lot of speculation in the West. When I was interviewed there, from their questions I could tell they had many preconceptions. I did not bother explaining. Film by nature is for society. I do not care how you perceive my films. But I really was not deliberately making up anything ideological; I did what my creative urge and my passion prompted me to do.

A film scholar has said that Ju Dou *was about incest, but Ju Dou does not have an affair with Tianqing until after she realizes that he has no blood relation with Jinshan.*
To put it simple, we did not intend to tell a story about incest. The original novel was about incest; Tianqing was Jinshan's biological nephew. Since we did not want to deal with incest, we changed Tianqing's role to that of an adopted nephew. The reason was that incest was not the theme of my work. As a matter of fact, I treat *Ju Dou* as the antithesis of *Red Sorghum*. *Red Sorghum* is about unaffected and unrestrained humanity: there are no rules, no imperial laws. It is about distortion and persecution. In other words, the hero in *Red Sorghum* has both the desire and the courage of a bandit, and the courage is stronger than the desire. The hero in *Ju Dou* has the desire of a bandit but no courage. Even if he has done something gutsy, he still lives in fear. He

feels like an underdog. In fact, one film is about freedom and courage, the other about humiliation and oppression. I reveal both sides of the Chinese. So, absolutely, it is neither incest nor classical Greek tragedy.

The classical Greek tragedy uses incest to preach about moral taboos. We do not want to present this simplified morality. We want to discuss the complementary sides of Chinese culture. We often say that had Yang Tianqing had My Grandpa's[9] temperament, he would have burned the dye mill a long time ago, killed that old man, and eloped with the man's wife. But his temperament is not like that; therefore, under pressure he acts furtively and humbly, hiding his real intention under an innocent front. If you exchange the dispositions of the male leads in these two films, you can see my point more easily. What I did in both films was characterization.

We talked about the simple primitive power of Yellow Earth. *This and all other Fifth Generation films have been overly interpreted.* Raise the Red Lantern, *for example, has been treated as an allegory of the Gang of Four.*
Some people's interpretations of our works overshadow the works themselves. It has been common for interpretations to impose themselves on art works.

Theory seems to have little influence on you, although when Li Tuo[10] and his comrades began talking about the reforming of Chinese film language, you did read some theory, correct?
Correct. But that was a short period lasting between six months and a year. Only during that period did we read seriously. Nietzsche and so on. That was it. It was very trendy in China then. To my knowledge, no Chinese director reads philosophy anymore. Philosophy is no more a part of our conversational topics.

Another issue is history. The biggest difference between Kaige and me is that I do not necessarily like historical themes, of which Kaige is fond. He is conversant with classical Chinese literature and fond of history. To me, history and the present are the same. The reason that I make more films about history is that historical themes are less censored. Although a strict system of censorship has existed in China for many years, there is some leeway in historic themes.

Even during the first years of the Fifth Generation, when filmic forms were considered the most important, many of your films were adaptations from literary works. What do you think of modern Chinese literature?

Literature today is not very good, worse than that of more than ten years ago. Literary circles will surely disagree with me, yet I am convinced of this. Because not only has the subject matter changed, but also the writers' egos have expanded. To put it bluntly, I find today's literature boring, without appeal. I am not saying that literature has to teach morals or connote some historical significance or responsibility. Ten years ago, when a new literature had just come into being, no matter what the subject, no matter if it was "root-search" [xungen] literature or "scar" [shanghen] literature, it was very powerful [the former searched in traditional culture the reasons for the ab-normality of the Cultural Revolution; the latter depicted the scars left on people's hearts by the revolution]. Today's literature is as boring as those city people who live under the influence of materialistic desire and money wor-ship. Sometimes literature becomes the property of a small circle. The more boring it is, the more it is considered by some people as pure literature. With such petty self-pity, literature becomes more and more maudlin, divorcing itself from the people and the interests of the broad audience and becoming something treasured by a small circle.

Today's China is unlike the West, which is post-industrial and postmod-ern. People in the West are really lonely and disappointed. Their loneliness and disappointment I feel is from their hearts. Today's China is boiling everywhere. No matter whether it is to gain power or to make money or merely to survive, the whole country is boiling, stirring, agitating. A big blowup, a dramatic change, even a volcanic eruption may take place. No matter whether the change is for the better or for the worse, it is unlike that in western society. Therefore, there's not much market for modern Western plays and performance art in China. What we see in Chinese literature is only self-promotion and the attempt to be fashionable. In today's China we see naked desire and craving everywhere. I am not judging this morally; what I am saying is that society is filled with instability and demands. A country of 1.3 billion people is now like this. Such a situation should excite literature and make it captivating, but it does not.

But the situation for film is the opposite of literature. Because of the stern, extremely stern, system of censorship that has been renewed many times, film has no room to breathe. Literature has much less restriction. With such freedom, if writers cannot turn out good works, it is the problem of the writ-ers. If we were given just a little freedom, if the control was loosened just a little, we could make much better films than the current ones. *Keep Cool* would have been a much better film had we been allowed to express what had been intended. Under the current system it became a facial façade without any essence.

Is it true that for the celebration of the 100th anniversary of the world cinema and the 90th anniversary of the Chinese cinema, none of the Fifth Generation directors were invited?
None of us were allowed to show up at the celebration. We are considered not as representatives of the Chinese cinema but as suspicious characters.

What do you make of this kind of mentality?
All this is temporary. This kind of political restriction will be removed sooner or later. In the long run I am optimistic. In ten, twenty, or thirty years, this kind of political, ideological restraint will be removed with the changes in society.

But an artist does not have so many years to wait.
That's really true. That is the misfortune for us.

People like you and Chen Kaige, who are well-known internationally, should be considered fortunate. It will be harder for the artists who are still considered unknown. Have you sen Lu Xuechang's To Grow Up *(Zhangda chengren)?*
Not bad, but it lacks any youthful and explosive impact. If it is to be the debut or the ground-breaking work for the entire Sixth Generation, *To Grow Up* falls short of the energy needed for ground-breaking work. Looking back now at *Red Sorghum* or *Yellow Earth*, they both have warm blood and life, which are missing in the works of the Sixth Generation. I think this is because the Sixth Generation was subject to practical considerations. It cannot be resisted: the need for money, the dilemma caused by censorship, and the awards at international film festivals. At a very early age the young people of the Sixth Generation knew much more and saw things more clearly than we did. Their aesthetics is much more expanded, as if there were a lot of different standards and contrasts. I think this is a bad a time of groundbreaking.

Maybe they are having a more difficult times than you did because when you were coming out, there were few good Chinese films; no big directors were there to block your way. Also, when you started making films, the studios were funded by the government; you could experiment as much as you wanted without worrying about the box office. They do not have such an advantage.

You cannot compare different historical periods. I do not think those objective conditions and circumstantial elements should be fundamental obstacles. I still believe a person's will can triumph over objective obstacles. I am a pagan who believes in human efforts. In my opinion there are more opportunities in today's China than ever before.

Including filmmaking?

Yes, because first of all, international society has talked about the Fifth Generation for more than ten years. They are sick of talking about it and are looking for the appearance of the Sixth Generation. Many foreigners who study Chinese films are eager—with an almost excessive enthusiasm—to help the Sixth Generation grow. Time and again they come to Beijing when a Sixth Generation film is still unfinished and watch the editing. They recommend the film to international festivals even before the film is finalized. Such enthusiasm and attention were not available to us. In addition, to tell you the truth it is not really difficult to find money in China today. It is much easier than finding money for film in the West. Some young people can casually develop a plan, get several friends, and begin to shoot. The Chinese media are the most interesting. They pay special attention to the novices. As a matter of fact, the domestic media have been more negative than positive to Kaige and me for the last few years.

Since the appearance of the Fifth Generation, haven't domestic critiques always been more negative than international ones?

The excessive coverage of the Fifth Generation has brought about the current negative opinion. A critic would say, "The endless talking about you has become so boring that I will make it a point to talk about somebody else." I don't think that the Sixth Generation has more difficulties. We are all under the same sky. If I did not accomplish anything more than ten years ago, I would blame no other person than myself for the lack of will, a will to succeed regardless of any obstacles.

Of course there is censorship. It was also very stern when we started. "Chairman Mao" and the "Communist Party" were still sung as "mainstream melody"[11] in *Yellow Earth*. Still, the film struggles and succeeded in presenting something of our own. That was what I meant by "strength."

That kind of strength can be generated. Even though one is restricted by politics under the political umbrella, one can sill bring out something fresh and powerful. What the current new generation still lacks in strength, this kind of power. Therefore, under the same sky they cannot create anything substantial, even with certain compromises.

Is it because they have not experienced the Cultural Revolution?
It may have something to do with that, but we cannot generalize. Maybe those younger than the Sixth Generation will be more powerful. I am not sure.

Are you suggesting that the Sixth Generation is not very talented?
Not necessarily. Judging by their works, I should say that they are quite talented. What they lack is will. In the last analysis, our first films were not necessarily the work of talent. I now firmly believe that, no matter what you pursue, will is needed—a strength from the bottom of your heart. Deliberate calculation is no good. Some Sixth Generation directors I know are too smart. They understand too many things; they are so well-informed about the outside the world and so familiar with the path to success that their filmmaking becomes an unemotional process. For instance, when they make underground films, at a very early stage when the films are being edited, they have already contacted foreign embassies and secured the channels to export the films.

When Kaige and I were making *Yellow Earth*, he knew little about the outside world, but he had an urge to talk about culture and history. At that time I knew this film would be outstanding. People say that it was the cinematography. No matter what, the director's intention was expressed, a very ardent intention. His emotions were expressed in a work that was supposed to serve contemporary politics. That to me is the most crucial. Now I judge a film not by how much philosophy it contains. The more philosophy it contains, the more I dislike it. I now revert to the most basic elements. When watching a film, I don't just watch how skillfully the story is told or whether the actors perform well; I look for the director's inner world, whether his emotions are strong, and what he tries to say. In his film we can discern his emotions, which, whether expressed in a tragedy or a comedy, will move the audience. That is what I call strength.

You cannot experiment for the rest of your life. Are you heading in one fixed direction?

I don't want to finalize my style too soon. But I think one cannot escape oneself, no matter how many changes one makes. This may be a rule, but I do not want to settle down too soon, nor do I want to deliberately formalize myself. I just want to do something new. If my current film does not differ from the previous one, I will feel bored from the beginning to the end. Freshness is the necessity of creation itself; I do not think too much about the rest.

Notes

1. The division of Chinese film directors has never been agreed upon, but the following is adopted by the majority: The First Generation (1905–1937) starts from silent films and ends at the beginning of the War for Resistance against Japan; the Second Generation (1937–1949) covers the War of Resistance against Japan and the Civil War; the Third Generation (1949–1978) starts from the Communist takeover of mainland China till two years after the death of Mao Zedong; the Fourth Generation (1978–1983) starts after the death of Mao and ends shortly after the Fifth Generation's graduation from Beijing Film Academy; the Fifth Generation (1983–1989) starts at their first film *One and Eight* and ends at the Tiananmen Square incident; the Sixth Generation (1989–present) is the new generation of the post-Tiananmen era.

2. Fifth Generation director, whose major works include *Yellow Earth* (*Huangtudi*), *Big Parade* (*Dayuebing*), *King of Children* (*Haizi wang*), *Life on a String* (*Ming ruo qinxian*), *Farewell My Concubine* (*Bawang nie ji*), *Temptress Moon* (Fengyue), and *The First Emperor* (*Ci Qin*).

3. Fifth Generation director, whose major works include *On the Hunting Ground* (*Liechangzhasa*), *Horse Thief* (*Daomazei*), *Rock n' Roll Youth* (*Yaogun qingnian*), and *Blue Kite* (*Zhangda chengren*). Tian Zhuangzhuang is a strong supporter of the Sixth Generation. After he was forbidden to make films, Tian became the producer for *To Grow Up* (*Zhangda chengren*), which is an important landmark of the Sixth Generation films.

4. With Zhang Junzhao as the director and Zhang Yimou the cinematographer, *One and Eight* is the first noticable Fifth Generation film.

5. Jian Qing, Zhang Chunqiao, Yao Wenyuan, and Wang Hongwen, the four Communist leaders considered responsible for the disastrous Cultural Revolution.

6. Written by Shi Tiesheng, *Ming ruo qinxian*, is a philosophical story and Chen Kaige further philosophizes it in *Life on a String*.

7. Qu Ying: the female lead in *Keep Cool*.

8. He Saifei: trained as a traditional Chinese opera singer. He Saifei played the third concubine in *Raise the Red Lantern*.

9. My Grandpa: the hero in *Red Sorghum*.

10. Li Tuo: a Chinese film critic, who in 1979 with his wife Zhang Nuanxin, a Fourth Generation director, published *The Modernization of Film Language*, which triggered a nationwide debate on how to rejuvenate Chinese film.

11. "Mainstream melody:" a catchy term invented by the Chinese Ministry of Propaganda to resist "politically incorrect" art works.

INDEX